SLEEPING GIANTS

AWAKENING YOUR SPIRITUAL INHERITANCE

JOHNNY NEWTON

Published by ONEFLO International Ministries
P.O. Box 431 | Bethel, Connecticut 06801
Book design copyright © 2016 by Sapphire Images. All rights reserved.
Cover design by Jennifer Newton

Published in the United States of America
All rights reserved.
ISBN: 0692765085
ISBN-13: 978-0692765081

ENDORSEMENTS

Working to create a spiritual resource for those looking to be informed and entertained, Johnny Newton challenges his audience to seek a fresh perspective with The Curfew Show. Newton's book *Sleeping Giants* is a compelling narration of ideas, insight, and experiences that could influence a generation. I highly recommend it!

Jon Leiberman
Radio And TV Veteran

Sleeping Giants by Johnny Newton is a treasure trove for your book shelf and a must read for today's society. It's a book about tragedy, triumph and principles that we can apply to everyday life. It speaks on procrastination, impartation, and revelation that will take you into the supernatural. I'm a hard person to impress, but this book gets a ten out of ten on my prophetic rating system. I encourage many to read this book at least twice you will be glued to your seats in amazement. I truly endorse this work of art.

Prophet Shawn Morris
Shawn Morris International Ministries

A spiritual life must follow a supernatural path! It will not have the same limitations or landmarks as a natural life. It will discover and release hidden treasures, lost inheritances and lead to many dramatic experiences. Such a life is reflected in Johnny Newton's spiritual auto-biography, *Sleeping Giants*.

In this book Johnny explains how he entered into his prophetic destiny as he obediently followed the leading of the Holy Spirit. He shares many nuggets of revelation he gained concerning angelic and demonic entities, communion, the blood of Jesus and generational blessings and curses along his prophetic journey. I recommend that you read his story prayerfully and expect similar supernatural results in your own life.

Joan Hunter
Author/Evangelist
Joan Hunter Ministrie

DEDICATION

For my brother Erik

TABLE OF CONTENTS

FOREWORD

Two things became very apparent to me as I read Johnny Newton's book "Sleeping Giants." One, here is a man who can clearly see into the spiritual realm, and two, he has an incredible gift and talent as a writer. Johnny writes in such an engaging way that it feels like you are right there alongside him. I love that! When I read the vivid descriptions of the spiritual realm, what it looks like, feels like and that whole dynamic, it rivals anything I've read about the spiritual realm. There are some powerful truths being revealed here but he tells these truths in a very compelling manner. It is a pleasure to read.

There are many "good books" that give us direction or spiritual truth or both, but there is something different about this book. There is an empowerment in this writing that is supernatural in my opinion.

From Johnny's early life of learning about the reality of spiritual darkness and the powerful struggle that lays unseen for most, to his discovery of his lineage, inheritance and ultimate destiny, Johnny shares his journey and what that can mean for us. The descriptions of spiritual realities and how they "work," and how we engage them either knowingly or unknowingly, is done with clarity and accuracy. It will be a great interest to all who really want to know how things truly work in this world.

Johnny covers many topics that might seem strange from a "religious" perspective like blood, DNA, quantum mechanics and more, but from a spiritual perspective they are essential for anyone who wants to know about navigating the spiritual realm. He weaves the story of his life and experience with scripture explained with greater depth you will ever hear in a church setting. I loved learning about his life and seeing what God has revealed to him and then learning those things myself.

This book is written in a level of spiritual awareness and knowledge that will affect you when you read it should you allow it to. Just like the way it really is, Johnny weaves the seen with the unseen and the natural with the supernatural so seamlessly that you can't help but get the picture.

Sleeping Giants is a very appropriate title for this work. All of us feel somewhere deep inside that we were meant for something greater. That there is something dormant inside that if we could just tap into it, things would never be the same. Many never get to figure out what that something might be. God has a plan, a special plan for each and every one of us. If you let it, this book may just show you.

Michael Van Vlymen

Author of *How To See In The Spirit* and *Angelic Visitations*

INTRODUCTION

I never used to like speaking in front of people. Standing up in front of my classmates to give a presentation for school was dreadful. Many times I would ask the teachers if I could just make the presentation after school or during a lunch hour. Sometimes I was accommodated, other times I was told that the exhibition was necessary in order to receive full credit for the assignment.

The stigma attached to speaking in front of people is actually quite common. In October 2014, The Washington Post released an article that stated that according to a study of American fears conducted by Chapman University, public speaking ranks number one as America's top Phobia. For me, it was not so much speaking and relaying the information, but more about the tremendous anxiety building up to the moment when I had to stand up and actually commit to doing it. Once I began the presentation I would relax and try to entertain the rest of the students. I figured that if I were able to make them laugh, even if I screwed up any of the information—or worse yet, flubbed the actual assignment—it would be much harder for anyone to notice. I turned these seemingly unnecessary presentations into performances.

Those initial demonstrations of novice composition led me into the bizarre world of professional wrestling. Years later I would find myself in front of hundreds, and sometimes thousands of people getting batteries and mustard covered hotdogs thrown at me, leaving me to wonder how I got into this situation in the first place. How I found myself in that world was because of my older brother, Erik.

Erik was a gregarious and larger than life person. He did things and lived his life unconventionally. His approach to life seemed so impractical to my logical way of understanding. Erik was a fan of professional wrestling his entire life, so it should not have surprised me the way it did the day he called to tell me that he was now the owner of his own wrestling federation. I remember thinking "are you joking? How can you save for your retirement doing that? Where is your health insurance going to come from, and who is going to help contribute to a 401K plan?" I could not have disapproved of the crazy idea any more than I did... that is until he asked me to be apart of it!

I was actually really surprised and taken aback by his offer. Erik told me that he knew I could "talk" and wanted to know if I would be interested in training to become a "manager." This got me thinking.

The manager's role in pro wrestling is a few different things: one of which is to get on a live microphone and get the crowd angry. The point in doing that is to incite an emotional response from the fans that gives them a story to follow. The evil manager has to drive the point home of who exactly the fans are supposed to rally behind. As a manager I needed to talk up the strength and talent of the crowd's hero in such a way that made them hate me, and then want for that hero to get his hands on me. The goal is to build a feud between a protector and a villain, and most importantly of all, to sell as many tickets to the shows as possible while the storyline builds. The manager's role continues on like this until the final showdown culminates to an end point where the fans' hero is victorious and the big mouth finally gets his comeuppance.

Every show I would put on a mask and business suit and play a pompous, germophobic aristocrat; a heel who took great pleasure in insulting the crowd as I arrogantly paraded around with the rightful champions gold title belt. There is much more to it than that of course, including a secret handshake and a strange coded carnival language. That is a story for another time.

Erik was fascinated with the idea of suspending your reality in order to follow a story that was obviously predetermined. He felt that I would be able to contribute to his company in ways that I could not see myself, opening a door for me that led to many other doors to be opened in promotions across the country. These open doors often led to more adventures than I could have imagined. I was able to perform and build confidence in speaking to mass amounts of people while at the same time running for my life! Many times I would have my safety threatened by drunken men in the crowd who felt I was disrespectful to the amount of teeth they were missing. Much of the storyline in the world of professional wrestling is a fabrication. However, many of the unscripted threats from the other side of the guardrail were very real. With every opportunity to perform came a different set of challenges.

A pastor once told me that he believed I played a villain so well because God was using these experiences to toughen me up for my calling, a time when I would take the mask off and speak about the reality of the supernatural kingdom of heaven. This same pastor told me that I was going to be "saying things to Christians that they wouldn't be ready to hear, and probably wouldn't like." As I look back, I really believe it was very prophetic. Actually, it was.

At the time I did not want to hear this word considering the fact that I was very upset with God. The years I spent running from him were out of anger and I was upset that my life was not what I wanted it to be. My existence spiraled down into a depression that was sustained and encouraged by a destructive lifestyle, which included drugs and alcohol. Working as a chef in the restaurant business, I often worked upwards of ninety hours a week without any form of break. It is very difficult to be happy slaving away in hot kitchens for almost no money. I was so unhappy with my finances, and wasn't pleased with my personal relationships either. So, I found it easier to just let go of certain responsibilities in my dispirited life, including my relationship with the Lord. I blamed him and rebelled by doing everything I was taught not to.

Working for my brother at the same time, I believed that Erik was toiling away at a ridiculous fantasy and I felt that I was in a way helping him waste his life. In my linear thinking I had all of the answers because I was the one working full time and trying to save for a retirement. In fact, I was actually just jealous that Erik was prospering by doing so little! It infuriated me because I would hear all of the prosperity preachers yammer on about the riches God has for me, yet here I was working like a dog with nothing to show for it. By my own choices I was ruining my life and shaking my finger at people like my brother who actually had it right.

It took a long time, but fortunately I chose to eventually seek deliverance from my destructive lifestyle and ask for forgiveness for my actions. I decided to change my thinking. Up until this point, everything I had been doing was incorrect and I started to realize that I needed to act upon the things that made me happy. I realized that I had to pursue the things that released endorphins into my brain in a holy and spiritual way.

In other words, I had to stop running from my calling.

Erik listened to the calling he had on his life and not only did he prosper, but he opened the doors for many other people to live out their dreams as well. He was obedient to the Lord despite how ridiculous it appeared to be on the surface.

It is only now that I realize that God is an unconventional God. He does things his way. Very often He moves in a way contrary to the way we think or feel things are to be done because we tend to approach things from a logical mindset, a way that dictates reason and form. We put things in boxes in effort to contain them as to convince ourselves into thinking we actually understand. Ironically, we only have a tiny understanding of the big picture. We limit ourselves and erect walls around the capabilities of our mind and we position ourselves as puny humans orbiting a sun within a vast universe. The truth, however, is that we are sons and daughters of the most high king of this vast universe. God is the master of eternity. We have a birthright that is beyond our manmade limitation of comprehension and we are made to do great and impressive things... things that only the offspring of the living God in heaven are capable of. You have both the right and privilege to come into alignment with the things that dwell in heavenly places.

People like my brother are the ones who are able to figure it out sooner than the rest of us. Those like my brother are the ones walk out their roles as diplomats of the kingdom heaven. When Erik went home to The Father in 2015, a veil was lifted in my mind. I saw how through obedience one man was able to awaken his spiritual inheritance and change many people's lives. I want to access those same gifts and show others the reality of a supernatural inheritance. I want those who are truly seeking the Lord to understand that our birthrights can be legally claimed from the supernatural and be used in the natural. It is time the enemy stops robbing God's children of what is theirs. The time has come to arise for the believers of Christ to step into their role as a kingdom colossus. It's time to awaken the sleeping giants.

CHAPTER 1

MISCALCULATION

"I demand human sacrifices!"

The hollow sound of her cold voice was dry and stern as it echoed throughout the arena. Before the singer could even finish her sentence, men, women, and teenagers rushed forward. Bodies began climbing over chairs and crawling on top of other bodies in a wave of excitement. A frenzied mass of people clawed closer to the stage. Thunderous cheers boomed in an instant uproar of jovial ecstasy. Those in the upper levels raised their hands in agreement.

A calm voice entered my mind, "Now you may leave." In my spirit I knew I needed to get far away, and quickly I made my way out of the concert.

• • •

About an hour before the show, I was in a good mood. The past week of work had ended and I now embraced the weekend with tickets for a popular band. The act was a musical juggernaut. They were touring the world on top of the billboard charts with their latest pop album. A buddy of mine and I made plans to meet up with two other friends at a hotel before heading to a popular New England casino. Since the casino was on the other side of the state, we decided to book rooms and stay there after the show. Just before leaving the hotel I took my cocktail of narcotics, carefully aimed to take effect at the start of the concert. Needless to say, my calculations were off.

The two of us jumped into our friend's car and headed to what turned out to be another forty minute ride to the casino. The closer we got, the more I knew something was off. I could sense inside that I was heading towards something awful, starting with a faint "thumping" sound. The noise was getting louder the closer we got to the arena. I tried to shake it off as best as I could until we were in the reservation. Yet, the sound was getting louder as we made our approach from the parking garage. The garage itself felt like a concrete labyrinth with the twists and turns of the many levels of the structure seemed to go on for an eternity. The grey walls were identical and it seemed like we were driving around the garage for a long time. Some of the lights were flickering and gave me the impression of a place you did not want to be late at night. I had the sensation of getting lost within it, and paired with not seeing any numbers or letters indicating which garage section we were in, I was quite certain that I would never be able to navigate the path back to the car later on.

Finally, we found a parking spot and started to walk up to the casino. As the automatic glass doors of the gambling den opened, the muted "thumping" sound I was hearing, instantly became louder and clearer: it was an Indian war drum. The unsettling tempo made me curious and I thought to myself, "I know this is an Indian Casino, but why on earth would they play this kind of intense beat over the sound system?"

The enormous orange colored walls cast a shade of which seemed very harsh to my eyes. As I looked around, I saw the mosaic turquoise patterns of Native American art everywhere. The geometric shapes seemed to be shifting in ways that made me think of how colors fall and move around when looking into a kaleidoscope. I wondered if the walls were LED screens because everything seemed to be moving.

The shapes and colors moved to the steady thumping of the Indian drumming... I even heard the drums in the bathroom! I stopped and just splashed water on my face to try and regroup my thoughts. Looking into the mirror and saw the glass vibrating in sync with the building drumbeat. I thought to myself, "wow, the speakers in this place have some serious bass." I left the bathroom and rejoined the group.

As the four of us made our way down the escalator towards the concert venue, I had to ask everyone else "do you guys hear those drums? Why are they so loud?" To which of course one of my friends replied "What drums?"

At that point I knew that should have taken my chances back at the parking garage maze and sat in the car for the next six hours. I was about to abandon my plans to attend the concert and do just that. I knew something was not right and I began to feel a nervous anxiety. We reached the bottom of the long escalator descent into the main area of the casino just outside of the concert area. I thought about making a move to the ascending escalator to the right, but instead, I did what many drugged up nuts would do, and I made a beeline for the beer stand.

The four of us entered the arena and split into two factions, myself and another friend had floor seats, while my other two friends were up on the second tier of the venue. As I made my way towards our seats, I could hear the drumming increase. I sat down and gazed up at the stage. The drumming stopped. As a matter of fact, everything seemed to stop. No one made a move and there was an eerie silence.

I looked at a stage decorated in what can only be described as a satanic catholic church: large, stained glass backdrops loomed high above a candle lit foreground. Rusted wire cages housed low wattage lamps, sprinkled about the stage next to the candles and reminded me of one of director Tim Burton's movie sets. It was very ornate and was certainly the most detailed stage I had ever seen at a concert. Part of me was impressed with the amount of peculiarity that went into the overall setup of decoration. I looked around the arena, and just as much as I was perplexed by the décor, the amount of people who had attended was equally surprising. Usually concerts fill up gradually, but this one was packed out well before the main act was scheduled to take the stage. Everything was moving in slow motion as the atmosphere shifted into a heavy, humid yellow haze. I looked over at my friend and speed and sound returned to normal.

In a nervous chuckle, the two of us both agreed how creepy the place looked and felt. The tiny blood vessels on the surface of my eyeballs began popping. I tried not to scratch at them to alleviate the itching sensation for fear of drawing attention to what my friend described as "glowing red" eyes. I wanted nothing more than for the house lights to go out so that the paranoia of a patrolling police officer or security guard noticing my clearly bloodshot eyes would halt. I had my sunglasses with me and I contemplated putting them on in an effort to disguise what I felt everyone was looking at. I decided that would look even more suspicious though, and immediately abandoned the idea.

After what seemed like an eternity of squinting and trying not to itch the lights went out. At that point, the fog machine kicked on, and I immediately saw what I can only describe as absolute horrors. I wanted nothing more than for the same house lights I begged to dim to turn back on.

IN THE COLISEUM

Neon red arrows shot down in small bursts like frozen ropes into people's backs and heads. Demon archers took aim at just about everyone on the floor below. Giant winged creatures flew high above the arena. Side to side, and back and forth, the scaly prehistoric beings made their rounds screeching and vomiting on people. To my right, a one-hundred-foot albino snake with the head of a man was constricting around those on the second tier. Choking those above, and at the same time, swinging to the ground floor and biting people. I saw its sinister grin completely enjoying itself as it gorged. Muscular purple demons wandered throughout the venue swinging their massive arms into people, and creating waves of torment. These satanic slayers were met without any resistance whatsoever as they cut through the crowd.

Although completely pummeled, the fans continued to rejoice and praise the lead singer. The front woman of the band was dressed in what looked to me to be the wicked witch of the west's wedding dress. She danced to and fro from stage left, to stage right. The dance movements came across as blatantly choreographed, and purposefully staged. It seemed slightly awkward as if it were an interpretive dance meant to be terrible on purpose, and I was actually taken back at how strange it looked.

The performance almost seemed like someone who was trying to recall the movements of what was supposed to be some form of ballet. However, as she was performing them, it was evident that the routine was a failure and thus turned comical. The awkward pirouettes, paired with the bizarre setting of the stage, and music, made everything appear as if to be some sort of ridiculous recital. Part of me wanted to laugh at how bad it looked, however something more sinister was happening that prevented me from doing so.

Amidst the singer's odd shuffle across the stage, she would sprinkle her fingers out to the audience. Neon red words emerged from the tips of her fingers and floated out into the arena. Words like "depression," "suicide," "cancer," and "poverty" bubbled through the air only to be snatched down by the jubilant crowd. Literally jumping out of their seats, the people desperately grasped at the words being peppered out from the singer's fingertips.

I knew the Lord had his hands on me. I could almost feel his hands resting on my shoulders. "My God is bigger, my God is stronger," I kept repeating. It was the only thing I could do to keep from not losing my mind to what was happening around me. It was so incredibly loud in the arena at times I couldn't even hear myself saying it out loud. I kept saying it over and over again. "My God is bigger, my God is stronger."

At one point the singer acknowledged it. I remember clear as day locking eyes with her as she glared across the arena over a sea of chaos. She looked at me and hissed into the microphone "No he isn't!" This of course was met with a thunderous cheer from the crowd despite not even really knowing what she was even referring to.

"My God is Bigger, my God is stronger" was the only thing I repeated.

During the lulls between each song, people would just be standing in place writhing like a snake. Their bodies twisted and contorted mimicking reptilian movements in sheer delight. I remember looking up and all around and realizing that I was completely surrounded by the craziest sight I had ever witnessed. Everywhere I looked, I saw a demonic army of beasts and creatures with total control over the ravenous fans.

The thought that entered my mind was "I wonder if it was this psychotic in the Roman Coliseum?" That is where I felt like I was, literally in the coliseum. I did not understand how these creatures could be doing what they were doing and the victims permitted it with great joy. What was really happening on a deeper level than just moving to the music was these fans who were enjoying themselves were agreeing and aligning with the dark powers. As they chanted in sheer delight, their spirits were getting clobbered by the onslaught of enemy manifestation.

I remember asking the Lord after every song, "Alright, can I go now?" I knew in my spirit that I was being kept there to witness the vulgar display of worship. It was also very clear to me that I was making terrible decisions in my life. This was most certainly a wake up call, and all I could do was repeat scriptures I had memorized over the years before I let my life slip out of control. Right before my eyes I witnessed principalities at work. Ancient evil beings that intrigued me in the bible were manifesting and I wanted no part of it. It was at this point when the singer arrogantly demanded for human sacrifices. She pointed out to the crowd and solicited the offering.

"I demand human sacrifices!" she called out.

Thousands of people readily volunteered. People pushed and dove over one another trying as hard as they could to get as close to the front of the stage as possible. The entire scene looked like a satanic altar call. I just sat in disbelief as what seemed to be the entire floor of the arena turned violently insatiable. Many of the people seated in the second tier of the building stood up with their arms stretched towards the stage. Their screaming and shouting sounded like a desperate plea and the guttural noises gave me the impression of a mass of people wanting to be chosen or picked for something special. Looking around, I saw many people leaning and reaching over the edge of the tiers that with one wrong movement would drop to the floor. It was then that I heard the voice of the Almighty say "Now you may go."

Turning to my friend, I said to him "listen, I can't explain this, but I need to leave right now." I stood up to head for the nearest exit and almost did a face plant. My legs were out of sync with my body, and I struggled to gather my bearings. I remember walking through the exit and feeling so incredibly relieved as if I had escaped some sort of disaster. This of course was yet another miscalculation on my end.

We left the concert and walked towards the exit gate

that led back into the casino. In front of the two of us stood a wall of about twenty-five police officers. At this point I figured I was toast. Here is a guy with glowing fire engine red eyes trying to maintain his equilibrium as he staggered his way through a gauntlet of police officers. I was clutching an empty plastic beer cup like a football. Could I be any more obvious?

My focus was on trying not to drop the empty cup as I staggered in slow motion back into the casino. There is no way the police officers could not have seen me, after all, it was the middle of the concert and no one was outside of the arena other than my friend and I. They either had no authority on the Indian reservation to stop me or I was supernaturally cloaked, I really do not know. What I *do* know is that anyone who is not blind could tell that I was in no way shape or form sober enough to be doing anything other than lying on the floor and questioning whether it was me or the room that was spinning.

It was as if the officers never even saw us. Not one of them even glanced in our direction. I had no real plan. I just knew that I had put distance between myself, the arena, and Johnny Law. If I could just find an exit, surely there would be a cab that could take us back to the hotel.

RAINBOW TUNNEL

We wandered through the casino desperately searching for an illuminated "EXIT" sign. Such a simple task is difficult in casinos, considering they are designed to keep people in so they will spend lots of money. After all, why would they want you to leave?

We wandered past row upon row of slot machines and bars. Lights flashed and bells rung as the sight of more creatures quickly drowned out the casino's sensory overload. Demonic entities protruding from the slot machines clutched a hold of the people who sat in front of them. Like zombies, the people sat in front of the one-armed bandits. They sat at the machines dumping money in without any emotion. Everyone seemed depleted like hollow cadavers. Some creatures had their hand grasp around the person's neck; others held cigarettes up to the mouth of the person. Horrific.

The casino itself is like one giant trading floor. The carpets have geometric patterns that remind me of a checkered playing board. Every time I have been in a casino, the people all look the same. They look that way because they are captives on that particular trading floor. The atmosphere is an exchange of freedom and joy, for that of addiction and torture. Patrons are seated at an altar and trade money for the hope of more money. The scheme of it all is nothing more than a perverse form of worship. The majority of people do not even win at a casino. I don't know about you, but I don't like losing.

The bars were the same. Strange looking smoke monsters jumped out of the liquor bottles and pulled people in, resembling drunken captives slumped on the stools. It was obvious to me that there was absolutely no joy in anyone. Not one person seemed happy. Even when someone at the slot machines won it was as if they were being punished. They sat at bars, craps tables, and video machines not at all phased by the circumstance. They looked numb in a way. Hollow, and numb. The saying, "sometimes the bar eats you" started making a lot more sense.

At one point we wandered through a tunnel of rainbow lights. The colored bulbs shifted and changed patterns as we walked through. I was mesmerized by it in a way because it seemed really beautiful, a far cry from the ashy smoke monsters and scaly creatures tormenting the people inside the casino. The tunnel took us into an arcade where there were many video machines and games of chance. There was also a daycare within the arcade.

I walked into the arcade/daycare and saw children playing and for the most part having a good time. There were a few who seemed afraid and I realized that some of the demons were hiding behind the standup arcade cabinets. The children were running around and the demons would trip them or pop out and push them over. I remember a few children crying. I looked over a plastic ball pit and lurking within it was some sort of wormy brown reptile, reminding me of the garbage creature in the compactor scene in Star Wars. I was terrified that one of the helpless children was going to go in the ball pit and get devoured.

It seemed like there were dozens of unsupervised kids in this place at such a late hour. I was overcome with sadness and thought about how people just dumped their kids off here so they could go gamble or do whatever they were doing in the casino. I looked over at my friend and said, "This is not where we are supposed to be." We went back through the Rainbow tunnel that seemed much more malevolent this time. The pretty colors seemed to change into harsh flashes of strobe light that made it difficult to navigate through. It was like staring at the bright light of a metal weld, a light that hurts and can damage the eyes.

I clutched the railing and put my head down as I trudged

through the tunnel back into the infested casino. In the old *Willy Wonka* movie, there is a strange scene where the characters are on a boat ride through the factory. The walls are changing with images of horrors and creepy things. When the movie airs on television now, it is purposely removed from the broadcast due to its graphic nature and is too scary for a children's movie. Looking back on the experience in the never-ending tunnel, that is what I am reminded of. Old Slugworth and all.

After what seemed like an hour of searching for an exit we made our way through a sliding glass door that gave way to a welcomed cool breeze. The night air was a relief from the smoky haze that filled the casino. Thankfully a black cab was waiting and we made our way towards the driver. Oddly, the cabbie was wearing sunglasses, which should have been a red flag considering it was around midnight. I told him where we were headed, and after a brief hesitation, the driver agreed to take us. "Finally," I thought to myself, "it's over."

Of course, I was as you may have guessed, I was wrong again.

BUMPER CARS

The ride from the casino back to the hotel turned out to be one of the longest car rides of my life. I had the pleasure of sitting directly behind the driver as we made our way to the hotel and the reason the driver hesitated became very clear very quickly. Attached to the man's head was a small blue demon that resembled a Pterodactyl, a winged dinosaur from the late Triassic period. Its features, however, were a bit more cartoonish; its eyes were a gross yellow color that stared back at me in anger. The creature clutched tightly to the driver's head, as its sharp talons dug into the man's brain. I could smell dope, and immediately realized that the driver was stoned.

As the car moved along, the cabbie began acting more and more strange. I could see the demon attached to the man's head moving its claws inside of his head. The movements caused the driver to act erratic. The man would slow the car down only to rev the engine and speed up unnecessarily. Many times during the trip he began tailgating the car ahead of us. I was able to see through the seat into the man's body. It was so strange, I felt like I had x-ray vision like Superman. I was able to see how the demon was interfering with the driver's neurological system.

The driver's right foot would react to the interferences he was experiencing in the supernatural realm. Sometimes the car would stop quickly as if trying to have the car behind us smash the rear end of the cab. Other times, the driver's foot would press the gas and zip through a stop sign. Each time there was a close call I saw twelve-foot angels outside of the vehicle acting as a buffer. They would step in and deflect other cars, or push us out of the way of a collision. I kept thanking the Lord for safe passage.

The entire ride felt like bumper cars at a carnival or an amusement park. Were never hit, nor did we collide with anyone else along the way, thank God. What reminded me of the amusement ride was the feeling, or anticipation of an inevitable collision. You ride in a car that is vulnerable from all directions. You become a 360-degree target! It was a remarkable experience to be able to witness such supernatural forces at work.

One of the very last things I recall from that night was leaving the cab and walking inside of the hotel. As we made our way to the elevators just past the front desk, I remember seeing a man behind the desk. I don't remember him saying anything to us. He just stood behind the desk wearing a bowtie and chuckled at us in a creepy, baritone giggle. At that point I was unconcerned with whatever that was all about. I just wanted to lock myself in a closet!

In the hotel room I sat on the edge of my bed in disbelief. I thought to myself, "there is no way to know how many times God protected and spared me on this night alone!" Only a God who was able to conquer death is able to save you from it. I am so grateful that the Lord has given me chance after chance to turn from my evil ways. I think back to the many situations and predicaments that I was able to walk away from and thank Him. What a knucklehead I was to think that I could get away with whatever I wanted. It was only a matter of time before I wound up on the wrong side of the coin. For that reason, I am eternally grateful that my time was not cut short for partaking in the screwed up life I was leading. Time and time again I was given another opportunity. I can say this unashamed because I am choosing talk about some of my experiences as a person who walked away from a generous God. I did everything wrong, and yet I had experienced His grace and redemption.

That night was a major turning point for me. I had to go through major deliverance to get free from the many hooks in my life. Untangling from the mess that one gets involved in is something that can only happen through total commitment to God. It is a process of cleansing and spirit rehabilitation. Some people do experience the radical cleansing and healing all at once, while others need to put work into pleading the blood over the areas of their life that need cleansing. Much of the pain we deal with are wounds inside of our heart. Parts of our spirit remain captive and chained in supernatural prisons. We have to cleanse those chambers and release the parts of ourselves from the torment that is taking place within our heart.

Maybe you have not delved into the same things I have, or maybe you have gone much deeper. There is no depth to deep to be saved. Ask the Lord to guide you through the channels that lead to the area of captivity and be set free. You are a spirit being that has access to the God's kingdom power. You do not have to waste time wandering around the supernatural realm where demons hang out. You yourself are an open portal to the glory realm of the King!

I was well aware of the spirit realm around me, but my focus had turned to that of the darkness. I now realize that our focus must be on the glory of the Kingdom Realm that we are granted access to. There is no need to waste time focusing on the evils in the spirit realm and fighting through it to get to the pure source. We as born again believers are an open heaven. The word says "In that day you will know that I am my Father, and you in me, and I in you" (John 14:20, *ESV*). That means that we are an open heaven. We have a direct and pure connection to God because there is no distance in the spirit. We have access to the clean paths of the Holy Spirit.

Jesus says in John 14:6 "I am the way, the truth, and the life: no man cometh unto the Father, but by me" (*KJV*). We use Jesus as the path through the spirit realm to get to the places within the kingdom of heaven. Jesus is the door we use. When we access the clean channels, we are protected from anything that the enemy can set against us. The more we use Jesus as the doorway, the more familiar we become with the proper routes to the places we have legal access to. Operating within the legal statutes that have been allocated to us prevent a person from going places where we are not allowed. Accessing these dimensions of the spirit must be done in the purified ways of the blood of the lamb so that we do not wind up at the mercy of the enemy.

Our God is a jealous God. If we desire a relationship with him, it is freely given. We do need to repent of sin so that we can invite him into our heart. This is pretty basic stuff, however it is so important to grasp and follow through with the fundamentals. Without an understanding of basic principles, it is impossible to build upon them. A strong foundation is necessary.

Later on in this book we will go much deeper into untangling and cleansing from the quantum levels of our bodies. We will talk about the importance of blood, and why it is so sacred. For now, I would encourage you to ask the Lord for a deeper relationship with him so that questions and concerns you have can be revealed to you, specifically in a way that makes sense to YOU. This book is a point of contact to come into agreement with the power of the Holy Spirit. I made the choice a long time ago to not only rebuild my foundation, but to start on a completely new plot of land, so to speak.

The gates of our body, that is the points of entry where we allow images and words to enter inside, must be cleansed and protected. The book of Exodus reads very clearly that in order to be saved from the destroyer that passed through

Egypt, blood was applied to the frame and doorpost of a person's home. There are doors that we have opened in our lives that need to be shut and have the blood of Jesus applied to so that God can move on our behalf. He can open up new gates for victory instead of defeat. If any of what I shared speaks to you, and you want to start the process of untangling yourself from the snares and hooks that are holding you captive, then I would invite you to repeat the following prayer:

"Father God, in the mighty name of your son Jesus, I come before you today humbly, and honestly. I ask for forgiveness of any and all sin I have allowed into my life. I take ownership and responsibility for my actions so that they can be absolved from my life by the blood of the lamb. I ask that you come into my heart today and guide me, as I build a relationship with you. I recognize the sacrifice that your son Jesus made on earth when he became the ultimate sacrifice for me. I know that he was put to death so that I may live. Lord God I ask that you cleanse the gateways in my mind, body, and spirit. Close any door that would allow the enemy to gain access into my life and open new doors for me to understand the ways of righteousness. I renounce anything I have ever put in front of you, as well as anytime I allowed sin to enter my life. Isaiah 60:11 says "Your gates will stay open day and night to receive the wealth of many lands. The kings of the world will be led as captives in a victory procession" (NLT). I want a personal relationship with you that yields victory and success over all that is contrary to the covenant you have made with me. Thank you for freeing me from the sin and death of this world. I honor you, and I glorify your holy name. Thank you father, In Jesus name, Amen."

CHAPTER 2

TIME

It's strange how sometimes you can look back at the horrors of living a desolate life and feel like it was a thousand centuries ago. Other times it can feel like just yesterday. I say desolate because that is how I felt, the empty and vacant feeling of wandering through a decade without moral judgment was a dry and barren season.

The aimless travel of a person who is gripped by depression is very lonely. I was searching just hard enough to only to find an answer in something that was easy. I say easy because it is easy to drink and get stoned. It takes zero effort to drop acid or trip out of one's mind on hallucinogenic drugs. When determined to fill a void with those particular things, it becomes very simple to give up on leading a productive life. Choosing to allow the mind to pursue whatever darkness is lurking in its subconscious as one feasts on a toxic buffet of psychotropic drugs becomes overwhelming very quickly. The result is either to go too far up the river and self-destruct completely or fight the way back.

I was so trapped by the poisons and toxins that I initially thought were helping me escape that I failed to realize that they were only multiplying my torment and holding me hostage. Fortunately, I was given chance after chance to turn from destruction. I was given the opportunity to leave that wasteland many times—God never gave up on me. He was very patient. Thankfully, I did not give up on myself and eventually chose to fight my way out of the trench. If not for the grace of God, this would be a different and more tragic story. Perhaps I never would have made it back down the river, so to speak.

One of the biggest lessons I took away from the experiences of living a deceitful life was that time does not stop. Meaning, the longer one indulges in the activities contrary to a righteous life, the longer the process of reforming the flesh to obey the spirit can take. The supernatural encounters as well as the entire episode as a whole at the concert became the last straw for me. Up until that point, I had tried my best to dismiss the previous warnings and close calls as best as I could. I found excuses to continue running from what I knew was the purpose of my life. Time did not stand still for me, and I initially found it nearly impossible to deal with the reality that I wasted so much of it. I had to get a grip on the fact that I needed to get it together and take some summer school classes in order to graduate out of the darkness I was in.

Forgiveness is one of the many facets of God that encompass his nature. He is big enough to forgive us of the transgressions that we have strung along for years. I understood that I had to seek him in order to break away from the grid of time. What I mean is that in the natural, or flesh, I had aged and lost "time." However, in the spirit, I was able to negate that loss and multiply it into a gain. God operates outside of what our mind understands the grid of time to be. He gives us grace.

Despite the disastrous years of what was shaping up to be a total catastrophe, my Creator's grace allows me to speak to people of the healing and redemptive nature of God. Scripture says in 1 Peter 5:10 that "the God of all grace, who called you to his eternal glory in Christ, after you have suffered a little while, will himself restore you and make you strong, firm and steadfast" (*NIV*). I don't think God's plan is to purposely make us suffer. I intentionally positioned myself in a place to receive the beating that came with that lifestyle. God is not the one who made me suffer; my continual choice to make those decisions took me down that path, just like it was Adam's choice to disobey God. He allowed sin into the earth by not listening to God's instruction. Even though the sin of that one man affects every person born, the obedience of another man named Jesus allows us all to become upright again. Romans 5:19 says that "For just as through the disobedience of the one man the many were made sinners, so also through the obedience of the one man many will be made righteous" (NIV).

It's His grace that allows my undeserving salvation. It's His nature to strengthen and equip us to deal with certain things once we have come to a place that we are ready to grow and listen.

Those years of pain are part of what has stretched me to maturity, or at least to a more mature point in my walk in Christ. These said years allow me to connect to people that have gone, or are going through the very same challenges.

27

Spending the time in that dark place has helped me to show others that God is in fact much bigger than any pain and torture we can endure. If we are willing to destroy ourselves, then that is our choice. But when we find out there is a living God who wants to know us at our worst so that he can bring us to our best, we encounter a tender feeling of redemption. Being received in an embrace of forgiveness and love is a magnificent feeling of restoration. Only God can restore the time we lose running from him. The call on our lives is uniquely different for each of us. When we choose to chase God, instead of our own selfish desires, God is more than capable of bringing the restoration of what we perceive as time lost.

Whenever we decide to grow our relationship, there is a time of nurturing. Time has to yield to God's everlasting grace before we can be strong enough for the next fight. Of course, just as with trees that bear fruit, pruning must be done continually. I accept this because without the hiccups and trials of experience, the perception of how minds formulate a logical schema of what His love is would then be altered. Such distortion exists as a diluted understanding of what, in actuality, is an unimaginable concentration of supreme benevolence and a love that never fails.

SUPER POWERS

People always say that time flies when you are having fun. Someone once told me that the same is true for those who are miserable. Ten years will fly by in the blink of an eye while a person lays in bed, too depressed to face the day. To some degree I thought they were right because the same happened to me in a way: an entire decade lost to depression and all sorts of horrors. Coming to terms with the fact that a good chunk of my youth was squandered was quite a tough pill to swallow.

Eventually I was able to get a grip on that, though, and realized that time is a fabricated box. Breaking out of the box and not allowing thoughts to get hung up on things out of our control is the key to freedom.

For many years I had been in a battle for dominion trying to master time. Ever since I was a child, wearing a watch would cause a reaction on my skin. I could get through about a day and a half before the itching started and then a red rash of bubbled sores would form a ring around my wrist. In effort to combat the lost battle of the watches, I started to try and train my brain to memorize or develop some kind of psychological power to always know what time it was at any given moment, a sort of coming in-tune with the universal time. If I could not master the watch, I would certainly master the time.

This concept was further engrained in me during my high school years; namely, during a chemistry class with whom the teacher casually mentioned that he never used an alarm clock. He disclosed that each night before he went to sleep he would say out loud and address his brain to wake up at a certain time. This teacher explained further that he would speak to his brain audibly the time that was displayed on the clock, and then simply command his mind to wake up at the exact moment he desired. Most likely unbeknownst to my teacher, this curious habit demonstrates that his words contain power and that he had taken authority over his flesh. The epiphany of this idea appealed to me not because I had bad experiences with watches, but because it alluded to a greater purpose.

That night before I went to bed I pondered my teacher's quirky habit. I began to think about the possibility of never needing an alarm clock. The most terrifying sound in the world is an electronic alarm clock ripping the mind from the sweet state of slumber. I understand the effectiveness of the sound but I disagree with the method of shock and terror when it comes to returning to consciousness. Being as I always read comics and wished I possessed some of the magical superpowers I read about as a child, I felt that ditching the clock could be achievable—although not nearly as magnificent as manipulating metal, or as sexy as x-ray vision!

Before I drifted off to sleep I looked at the clock and spoke aloud what time it was. After doing so, I spoke to my brain and commanded it when to wake up. At 6:15 in the morning, I awoke five minutes before my alarm clock went off. I began to take authority over my brain more after what I determined to be a complete success of the experiment. I figured that if my mind knew when to wake me up, then surely my internal clock was accurate enough to know the time at any given moment of the day.

For years after that I had abandoned all forms of external devices. My mind had sharpened with the ability to move beyond just a predictive approach to flat out knowing the exact time. The development was astonishingly acute. Yet, that all changed when cell phones became the norm. I remember when cell phones were on the rise. They evolved quickly and soon had an external screen, and later became one slim HD screen. The first thing we see when we look at our phone is the time. Very quickly I became just like the vast majority of the planet by becoming a mobile communicating member of the Twitter age, thus letting my "mutant power" whither.

What is my point? We are so easily enslaved by *things*. We willingly allow distractions like technology to dictate many areas of our lives. The word of God says in 1 Cor. 6:12 "'I have the right to do anything,' you say--but not everything is beneficial." I have the right to do anything"—but I will not be mastered by anything. Do not be mastered by anything, including time!

We are not of this world. We are spirit beings living in a body of flesh and bone. It is why we should not allow ourselves to be subject to time. The reason why I can say that with the utmost confidence is because of what is written in the book of Jeremiah. The word says "Before I formed you in the womb, I knew you..." (vs 1:5). That means before God made or formed our bodies, he knew us. That tells me that he knew our spirit before he formed the shell to house it.

My personal belief is that the Creator formed us in Heaven and then sent us to earth to walk out and perform our mission. Some people use the term "calling," I like to think of it like a special forces operative. We are briefed in Heaven and sent to accomplish what was assigned to us. That is the reason for our gifts and talents. They are to be pursued and developed in order to aid us in achieving our purpose—our very own super powers!

I also believe that we are not subject to the law of time because we can command it to stop. What does that mean? It means that we base what we think we know about time on the two great big visuals in the sky, the sun and the moon.

31

The earth rotates around the sun once every calendar year while every 24 hours, it spins in a faster rotation. Although there are some people who believe that this theory is hogwash. They believe NASA is covering up certain facts and that the earth is in fact flat. If you don't believe me, just Google it!

There is a thriving community of people who disagree with what the world governments say is truth. I do not know for sure because I have yet to see planet earth from a point of view that is further than that of a window seat of an airplane. So until I do, I cannot say what is right or wrong. To be frank, I don't actually care either way. What can be said as fact is that most of us believe that one day equals 24 hours and thus confine ourselves to that number. This becomes a problem because when we restrict ourselves to these limitations, the enemy has an easier time accomplishing his agenda.

When I read the book of Joshua, it states clearly that Joshua was able to control the day by speaking to the stars. As he commanded them to be still, the word states this: "So the sun stood still and the moon stood in place until the nation settled their score with their enemies. This is recorded, is it not, in the book of Jashar? The sun stood in the middle of the sky and seemed not to be in a hurry to set for nearly an entire day" Joshua 10:12-13 (*ISV*). How amazing is it to know that when we are properly aligned with the written word of God, that we have the potential to freeze time.

I love this story because the Amorites are fleeing from Joshua and about to escape into the night. Joshua is able to exercise his right as a Son of God, a spirit being who can access the supernatural power of El- Shaddai. In turn, we can take authority over anything that stands in the way of conquering our enemies. When we recognize our authority and walk in line with the decrees of the Lord, we are synced with the power to stop the sun from setting! If that isn't a super power, I don't know what is.

It seems incredibly farfetched to think that we can stop time. Taking a step back to realize why this seems so unbelievable, the gateway opens and freedom starts to manifest into an excitement of its possibility. We have to understand that we enter a broken world only to be raised to believe thousands of years of agendas, false doctrines, and complete lies! We are born into sin when we enter earth, not that we have sinned at birth, but we are born into a lifestyle of sin.

In addition to the fact that we cannot yet speak, our motor skills are not well developed. The reason for our arrival is quite literally impossible to articulate in any way to anyone what our purpose actually is. As earth moves further along the timeline away from our spirit's mission briefing, we are pummeled by the harsh and sinful nature of this fallen world. Before we know it, we are forgetting our purpose for even being here. Things start to really get tough because just when we think we have it all figured out, we are thrown into a totally new environment with a new set of rules and structures. We wake up one morning expecting to enjoy another day of the familiar, only to be swept away and sent off to where the lies begin: an unfamiliar place that offers group snack time and naps, a place that promises the opportunity to learn and be educated, and a place that is the start of our supposed future. We look around the colorful room and the next thing we know a much taller person stares us in the face, smiles, and says "welcome to kindergarten."

LIES, AND THE GREAT ELF ESCAPE

The very first thing I remember being taught in school was a memorization lesson about "Home." Specifically, what my address was. From day one people want to relegate us to this planet. Innocent in nature, in case of a very possible abduction or some other terrifying scenario that was actually used to scare us into remembering where our home was, the underlying effects are quite sinister. Immediately as a child we are being implanted with fear triggers. The fact of the matter is that as a spirit we have dual citizenship in both Heaven and Earth. We are servants to the master of eternity, the Lord God whom we were created in the image of.

Our God trumps time by being bigger than the imaginary boundaries and rules of time that have been set up to fence in and sustain control. God does not have a beginning or end, nor is He something that can be measured, nor subject to man made rules and limitations. We as children of the most high have that same birthright. This means that we, too, should not be subject to time and the constraints that the celestial bodies put on our lives—and I do not just mean horoscopes. If we are in Christ and He is in us, then we in spirit are beyond the limitations that we willingly have allowed to confine us.

As a youngster in school, the second thing I remember being taught was the clock. I vividly remember a giant cardboard clock face with moveable hands. Almost immediately upon attending kindergarten, children are told the function of the big hand and the little hand. The only hands we need in this life are the two big hands of God—blessing and favor! One hands clears the obstructions to open doors, as the other is placed to help guide us through the turbulence of this realm. The Bible even says, "Do not be conformed to this world, but be transformed by the renewal of your mind, that by testing you may discern what is the will of God, what is good and acceptable and perfect" Rom. 12:2 (*ESV*). The sooner we realize that we are not subject to being quarantined to what is only visible with the natural eye, the sooner we can start to move and operate in levels beyond this three dimensional planet.

A child's faith is very pure. Children are so much closer on the timeline to their origin of heaven and have not been distracted or lied to. They can still believe wholeheartedly in what many adults scoff at. I believe that is why Jesus loves children so much. The Word says in Luke 17:6 that "If you had faith even as small as a mustard seed, you could say to this mulberry tree, 'May you be uprooted and thrown into the sea,' and it would obey you!'" (*NLT*). It takes very little for a child to trust and believe what is possible. In fact, the Word of God also says "But it is the spirit in a person, the breath of the Almighty, that gives them understanding. It is not only the old who are wise, not only the aged who understand what is right" (Job 32:8-9 *NIV*).

The lies of adulthood often times deflate and derail the faith of children. How often do we downplay the example of monsters in the closet? Adults quickly dismiss the notion that there is a boogeyman lurking beneath a bed and children are labeled with an "overactive imagination," when in fact children are incredibly receptive to the supernatural and may actually be seeing very real things.

To further illustrate this point, exploring what appears as "innocent" toys and dolls reveal what can be classified as actually satanic idols that carry impure things and cause children to react to the atmosphere they carry. These toys may be packaged in fun boxes and playful shapes but are nothing more than miniature neon colored beacons and demonic magnets for spirits to congregate around. The world is full of these traps set up to ensnare children at the earliest age possible.

This is why I witnessed demons inside of the casino arcade. One of the ways they have access into people's lives is through video games and games of chance. Avatars in games are more than just harmless play. They are actual representations of a person in a different created dimension. At the time, I could not understand how the creatures could be in the arcade/daycare harassing the children. Not only were they really real, but they were able to take advantage of the children. Kids are able to manipulate the gates of imagination so easily because they have not been beaten down and lied to as much as an adult has. They are very receptive to the supernatural world.

Growing up, my siblings and I had access to the latest video games and action figures because of the generosity of our grandparents. We grew up in a neighborhood that was surrounded by family and much of our childhood was spent at our grandmother's and great grandmother's houses on each side of our own house. We figured out very quickly how to angle for the latest toy or video game and our attempt was always met with success!

I remember one video game in particular I had when I was a child. One of the characters was a tiny elfish looking man who carried an axe to use as a weapon. I remember my great grandmother saw me playing the video game one day and told me to turn it off because she had seen that elf before. I did not understand what she was talking about because I rarely played the game, let alone at her house. She explained to me that one evening she awoke in the middle of the night with leg pain. She looked down and there crouching on her legs was the same elfish man with an axe from the game! She rebuked the demon on her leg and pled the blood of Jesus. When she did that, the elf man was terrified and jumped off her legs and ran straight into the television set. Notice that the demon escaped into the television.

Televisions are gates. It is important to guard those gates and restrict what is allowed to enter into the home. They are called channels for a reason! Each one is a path that allows either good or evil into the home every time we stop and devote our attention to it. Be mindful of what you are allowing to have access into your home.

When I heard my great grandmother tell me about the great elf escape of 1989, I of course was frightened and I took the video game, the poster it came with, and everything else related to the game that I owned and threw it into the fireplace when I got home. I knew that it was dangerous— and evil—and that I did not want it anywhere near me!

As an adult, I know now that the blood of Jesus covers me. I also know to take authority over my surroundings and ask by faith that gates such as televisions, cellphones, and computers be cleansed in the blood of Jesus Christ. Many of the characters found in cartoons, television, and toys are in fact idols. They are disguised as lovable neon colored monsters or figures. The truth of their nature is much more sinister than their appearance. And this isn't a witch-hunt; this is something that came out of an encounter with God himself.

A few years ago, God revealed to me in a dream some of these entities. In the dream I was watching what looked like baseball cards or tarot cards cycling one by one in front of me like a carousel. On each card was a picture of the character along with stats, or information, about the spirit in operation behind each figure. The cards would cycle around and stop on a particular character. The card would illuminate and rise up from the bunch. An audible voice would say "that's a demon." I could see the information and purpose of the demon's assignment. Then the card would lower back into its spot and the cards would continue to cycle through. They were characters and illustrations that I recognized in commercials and cartoons.

This is not legalism nor is it someone being hypercritical about what is evil. This is someone who sees into the spirit and understands that good and evil do exist, and more often than not, evil likes to disguise itself as something good (2 Cor. 11:14).

The enemy is very clever and knows how to try and get his hooks into people as early as he can. He is a master marketer and uses characters and seemingly innocent personalities to infiltrate the camp of the righteous. If it was obvious, we wouldn't think twice, but something coated in fun colors and a cute face makes us quickly think it's harmless. I recommend a fantastic book "Bound To Lose, Destined To Win" by evangelist Curtis "Earthquake" Kelley. In his book, Kelley goes into detail about dolls and action figures literally coming to life almost like a satanic "Toy

Story"! What is really interesting about the book is that Kelley grew up and writes about a town nearby my hometown. I find his book to be very credible, not only because I have witnessed similar things, but also because he talks about real people that I have met—and I have never met Kelley.

It's important to ask God for a discerning spirit in life, especially when it comes to what we allow our children to be near. The bible talks about idols and pagan statues many times. I do think that many of these children's toys and dolls are just modern day idols. Time as we understand it, goes on and these things just reinvent and rebrand themselves in clever new ways to get their hooks in deeper. To combat this, we have the gift of the blood and it is our right to let this blood cover over our lives and the things we allow in it.

Tying in all of the concepts of this chapter, my sister had an unusual encounter with video games and the characters in them. One video game that she liked in particular was a role-playing game that has grown to be a popular franchise. There were different portions of cities in this game that one could visit and explore and talk with the characters that inhabited them. Though innocent in appearance, the power of the imagination creates a pathway of engagement with enemy traps.

She had been playing the game over the course of a couple of days when she felt that she needed to stop because there was something unclean in the game. In disobedience she continued to play and with the character she was role-playing as, she walked into a potion shop.

Let me just stop for a moment and explain what was happening here. My sister, as a human being, was playing a *video game.* She was not the character, but she was using the avatar to engage this created reality. This games universe was the manifestation of someone's imagination. It was not a reality we could engage with our physical bodies, but we could engage it with our spirit through the gateway of the imagination.

Anyway, she walked into the potion shop an immediately she perceived something jump out of the television and latch onto her shoulders. The spirit of fear was tangibly heavy and caused panic. She eventually had to undergo some deliverance to remove the burden of that demon spirit. Thus my point is demonstrated that even "altered realities" carry no distance in time or space and that one needs to be careful in what he or she allows entrance into the atmosphere.

These things that we have been taught as a child to engage have become more real than reality itself. The hologram of "innocence" begins at a young age, and just like the lies of time, we believe and accept them as reality without the awareness of the complications that result. Solving this corrupted file we have been processed with does require untangling, but not necessarily with a Catholic priest and a bottle of holy water. Instead, we call upon the power of the blood of Jesus.

CHAPTER 3

HEMOGLOBIN

I am laying some important foundations for what I believe to be necessary in order to awaken your spiritual inheritance. We talked about breaking away from the mindset of time restraints and limitations, specifically pertaining to the "loss" of it. We now know that God is able to not only restore the time lost or wasted, but willing to turn that loss into a gain. Just as we need to renew our minds and begin to understand time differently, the same goes for blood.

God has shown me the importance of blood, and it's through faith and common knowledge of the Word of God that we know that we are cleansed in His blood. Why blood though? Because "the life of the flesh is in the blood, and I have given it for you on the altar to make atonement for your souls, for it is the blood that makes atonement by the life" (Lev.17:11 *ESV*). We have forgiveness because Jesus became the ultimate blood sacrifice for us on Calvary. His blood was shed on the cross so that we could have life in ours. It was this selfless act that enables us to be free from the chains and bondage of unforgiveness. We repent of any transgressions using Jesus as the gate to the Lord. Jesus made it possible for atonement by allowing us by faith to lay those sins on the cross, never to be held against us again.

Blood has a voice. Genesis 4:10 states "[God] said, "What have you done? The voice of your brother's blood is crying to Me from the ground" (*NASB*). When Cain murdered his brother Abel, the blood shouted to its Creator for justice. Cain's DNA recorded his actions and thus passed down that curse to his children. The Bible talks substantially about such curses being passed down through one's lineage. For example, the disciples asked Jesus in John 9:2 who sinned that caused the man's blindness, him or his parents. So sin takes record in our physical DNA.

Parents even named their children after curses. In 1 Chron. 4:9-10, it states:

> "Jabez was more honorable than his brothers, and his mother named him Jabez saying, 'Because I bore *him* with pain.' Now Jabez called on the God of Israel, saying, "Oh that You would bless me indeed and enlarge my border, and that Your hand might be with me, and that You would keep *me* from harm that *it* may not pain me!" And God granted him what he requested." (NASB)

Jabez is cursed and labeled with the name given to him; however, he pleads with his Creator to spare him the pain he is named for. God hears this request and honors Jabez with a life contrary to the pain and sorrow he was named to have.

Blood is also code. It is holy coding of life to be exact. DNA strands can literally be read and interpreted through this code to show genealogical patterns and makeup. Blood is like a supernatural script of both blessing and curses that are passed down from generation to generation. Scientists and Medical research confirm this. That is why when one sees a doctor they ask of family medical history and repetitive illness. Insurance companies know this, too.

As we springboard into a progressively medically conscious world that is consumed by profit, we will see the increase in genetic testing. This caution will become more of a requirement. Although passed of as preventative diagnosis, we as spirit-led Christians should be aware of how clever the enemy is. Don't think for one second that an insurance company will be unbiased and not use that information to charge a higher premium for those who happen to have a certain gene and predisposition to certain diseases. Pharmaceuticals are a cash-cow business and insurance companies have their hands deep in the pot, also.

Even more importantly to be aware of is not what the doctors and scientists say is within your cellular makeup, or "potential risks," but where we lend our agreement to. Our words have power and death and life are in the power of the tongue (Prov. 18:21), and we choose life or death based on what we nod "yes" to and say "OK" to at the doctor's office. Remember that we do not answer to the word of man. We answer to a higher source—the *highest* source! When someone speaks illness or disease over your life, it is important to be aware of what you allow to be spoken over you. There is great power in words.

When we have someone speaking sickness over our body,

we have two choices: to agree with the word curses—which is exactly what that is, curses being spoken—or we can take a stand and rebuke the enemy's attack. Stand firm in the word. Plead the blood of Jesus over yourself and put on the whole armor of God. Speak cleansing over your cellular makeup. Take authority over your DNA and RNA strands all the way down to the quantum levels all the way back to Adam. Command restoration and re-alignment beyond what can be measured by science. And most importantly, repent for the sins that you committed and the sins of your blood line all the way back to Adam.

Blood is made up of light and sound. Genesis tells us that in the beginning, God spoke "let there be Light." With his vocal chords vibrating inside of his larynx, God caused *sound* waves to manifest into light. When a person begins to take action over the flesh, the governing spirit can have easier access to the glory of God. The healthier your body becomes, the more it mirrors your spirit, as stated in 3 John 2. It is the spirit that should be in control and not the flesh, hence "spirit led."

Science has also begun to prove this theory in that blood is congealed light. Interestingly, only liquids that contain matter have the capability of congealing. Light is the only substance that exists that is both a frequency and matter. Furthering the research, scientific findings have begun to exhibit the ability to communicate through light, which has ironically been in the Bible for millennia. Blood as congealed light then carries the record of sins and curses from generation to generation and must be cleansed in order to exhibit the fullness from our spirit. Of course, this can only be done through the blood sacrifice of Jesus. Science is finally catching up to the scripture!

CHEFING IT UP

As stated previously, blood is code and therefore can be read and interpreted. I believe that the blood records as well. Take for instance muscle memory; although I do not play the guitar anymore, I can after many years still pick up the instrument and make the finger shapes to play chords. Do I have the strength and dexterity to play for hours? Of course not. However, my hands and fingers know automatically where to go without even thinking. Those actions and movements are recorded within my body. The muscles have "memory" because of repetition. I believe if the blood can record these mundane, procedural movements, then surely it would record adverse contact with our cellular structure.

We know that Abel's blood recorded the flesh's demise when Cain murdered it. This means that information transmitted to our cellular makeup by means of trauma, or blunt force should very well be encoded. Take for instance a cut wound, or burn. I have many scars and brands from years of working as a chef that to this day still have sensitive areas when touched because of damage to the nerves. I believe that the same is true for animals and this is also one of the main reasons why I am a vegetarian.

When an animal is killed for consumption, the pain and trauma is documented within the flesh of the creature. Understand that the lives of cattle, chickens, and every other animal that is raised for the industrious purpose of food, is miserable. The memories of the horrors of their life and death are encoded within the flesh. Once ingested into our bodies—much like antibiotics and hormones—the DNA makeup that carries the record of trauma and fear are absorbed into our systems and can cause adverse effects in our own genetic structure. Studies now show that certain foods like red meat, hot dogs, and pork now cause cancer!

Listen, I am not trying to make anyone feel guilty because they eat meat. If you do, then great, I think you are just fine in my book. My purpose for writing about this is to explain what happens to these animals as they become dinner in relation to the blood and what we ingest. It is always important to "bless" your food. I believe God has the power to cleanse, and transform the cellular structure of animal proteins if you ask him to. It's a matter of engaging with the spirit and commanding the cells to do so. Often times you find that it usually takes slightly more than a "Rub a-dub-dub, thanks for the grub, amen" is all.

Years ago, God used a secular video to illuminate what was already on my heart from what I had witnessed in my own experience. Being a chef, I was constantly working with animal flesh. When dealing with high volumes of food for restaurants or corporate facilities, cooks encounter the end result of a terrible existence. Most people enjoy going out to dinner and have a good time never thinking about the process that is involved from start to finish. People see the meal in a stage that is ready for consumption, yet never see what an 18x18 inch box stuffed with a dozen chicken carcasses looks like. The shattered bones of the animals are packed into the box swimming in blood and innards. People do not know, or care, to see just how cruel the food industry is to animals.

During an internship in Manhattan, I was working for a

world famous celebrity chef who had a lamb chop entree on the menu. One of the shipments of lamb came in and was from a different vendor than the kitchen normally dealt with. The mangled chops arrived smashed into a tiny box, mutilated in order to make them fit snugly for transport. The chef looked into the box and I thought he was going to be angry that the product he bought was unable to be used for the dish he had on the menu. My instinct was that he was going to be upset that he just spent money on an expensive protein that could now only be used for a stock or soup. Instead, he looked down at the lamb and responded with something that really struck me. "It's obvious these people aren't animal lovers," he said in a dejected tone. He then walked away with somewhat of a somber countenance.

Thinking to myself, I remembered that this man is a carnivore. He eats meat. He serves it to his patrons. Yet, he has enough compassion in his heart to understand that animals have a life and that they are living beings as well. Some are raised only then to be killed for consumption. Even in death, their remains are violated. This was a problem for me and is even mentioned in Proverbs 12:10, where it says "a righteous person cares [even] about the life of his animals, but the compassion of wicked people is [nothing but] cruelty" (*GWT*).

As I stood at my stainless steel workstation scraping the ribs of the chop with a paring knife (French cuisine demands that the bones are a pristine white after roasting), I thought about the misery of the animal's life. I thought about why this task I was performing was necessary. I thought about having compassion and wondered why I participated in the genocide of life that was not really needed. A high-end meal, I thought, all in exchange for a low-quality life.

BLUNT FORCE TRAUMA

I love the book of Daniel. In it, the bible talks about a meatless diet. Chapter one goes into detail about how Daniel, Hananiah, Mishael, and Azariah ate only a diet of vegetables and water for a season. After the end of the term, it was clear that Daniel and the others were healthier and more nourished than those who ate of the King's royal food. God then rewarded Daniel the gift of dream and vision interpretation, as well as granting each the four men understanding that exceeded the knowledge of any of the kingdom magicians by ten times!

The prophetic gifts Daniel operated in were multiplied after the "choice" foods were removed from their diet. I really believe that those who move in the same anointing stand to increase the level at which they work with the adoption of such a diet. It is a tremendous key in operating at our full potential. Job 33:14-18 even tells us:

> "For God does speak- now one way, now another- though no one perceives it in a dream, in a vision of the night, when deep sleep fall on people as they slumber in their beds, he may speak in their ears and terrify them with warnings, to turn them from wrongdoing and keep them from pride, to preserve them from the pit, their lives from perishing by the sword."

God often uses our dreams to speak to us for many purposes. A clean diet aids in the interpretation and understanding of what he is conveying to us. It builds our confidence and ability to understand His message to us by way of increasing our intellect, perception, and discernment. It builds our ultimate trust in His word by strengthening our faith. An animal protein based diet includes the stress, trauma, and negative side affects that the creature endures from birth to slaughter. The way our government allows God's creatures to be confined, transported, and destroyed creates an atmosphere of suffering for the animal right up until its slaughter—and some countries deliberately create such an atmosphere to alter the structure of the meat. I believe the blood records all of that.

Think about it this way, many of the animals we eat are kept in stalls preventing them from any movement, causing emotional and physical distress. Animals in such conditions are prone to blood clots and sickness. Living in their own feces, they are given a diet of hormone and antibiotic-filled food for their entire existence that often does more harm than good. All of this suffering leads to one of many forms of slaughter. Some animals get their throat slit and hung upside down, while their flailing bodies go into shock as they bleed out. Some are lucky enough to get a pneumatic rod shot into their brain, while some just wind up getting whacked in the head a few times with a sledgehammer. This is not fun and games, this really is how the food industry deals with processing meat. Of course there are small businesses that offer a humane environment for their animals, but very rarely do those meats end up on the grocery store shelves. And even so, not every business practices what they preach, and a claim of humane treatment may not be what we would necessarily call humane.

It really is a gruesome reality that such traumas are recorded into the animal's DNA. The brain is a super-powered organ that governs the memory and the functions of our bodies. Messages through the Central Nervous System determine which enzymes are released at what times, and if the brain has the power to send messages of distress, then it also has the power to encode messages in the DNA. A basic study of the body's cellular functions shows that even down at the core of the cells, the nucleus, DNA can be altered and changed by messages sent from the brain.

Interestingly, when we eat food we are also interpreting the messages carried in our food's DNA. There is much controversy surrounding the genetically modified foods (GMO's) through pesticides, but pesticides come from some of the amino acids found in our own DNA. If the issue then with GMO's is a restructured set of aminos that causes harm to the body, and our brains have the capacity to do such a thing as alter our DNA, emotional and physical trauma are a bigger power player than people give credit. Whether GMO's or trauma-altered foods, none of which is anything I want to be ingesting. Again, just remember to say your "Rub a-dub-dub's."

As a chef I saw this everyday. Why do you think there are so many recalls? There are products, and meat, that get recalled what seems like every week in the food industry. Some recalls the general public probably will never even hear about. Consumers have to trust that the restaurant they frequent is both aware of, as well as complying, with safety notifications when it comes to the constant contamination of meat. To me, the health risks alone are enough to avoid certain foods.

The fact of the matter is that the people in charge of the meat industry are obviously not animal lovers. Considering the treatment they advocate for livestock, it tells me that they are not people lovers either if they are comfortable with consumers eating the poisons and toxins that are fed to the animals. The bottom line is that the blood was created for life, not to befall a gruesome death.

Again, I am not trying to make you feel guilty or angry and I am not trying to convert you or change your diet. I understand that hunting was, and may still be necessary for some people, as well as for population control etc., just NOT for sport. I think personally that killing for thrill is not only gross, but is self-congratulating and small. I am simply illustrating what I believe to be an important issue that widely goes unchallenged. I hope this sparks a realization that mankind has been given dominion over animals and therefore have a responsibility to protect them and steward them in their best interest. I delight in Psalm 36:6: "Your righteousness is like the highest mountains, your justice like the great deep. You, LORD, preserve both people and animals" (*NIV*).

All this is to illustrate the power of blood and the importance of the blood sacrifice. The Old Testament has many examples of Blood sacrifices. It tells us that the blood of an animal offering was to be shed and splattered on the altar of the Lord's temple. Blood is a serious and holy offering to the most high. Animal blood is no longer necessary because Jesus's blood was shed and splattered from his own body. His body, or temple, was the last and supreme blood sacrifice for us! That is why we as believers are able to plead the blood of Jesus and are completely set free from the death penalty of sin. His blood was shed on this earth with the eternal memory of the suffering on Calvary so we could be granted salvation. This powerful blood allows us to be cleansed of transgression in order to further the Kingdom's advancement here on Earth. The blood cries out Amen!

BLOOD SACRIFICE

God cares for both humans and animals. Why else would he have saved them from the great flood and placed them in the ark with Noah? Our blood needs to be set free from the toxins and impurities that not only come from the slaughter of animal protein, but also the generational curses that pass down from parent to child.

Isn't it strange how people always say "poverty breeds poverty?" It is actually a curse. Poverty is lack. We serve a King who is all about abundance! So why then do those born into poverty, stay in poverty? Somewhere along the line, a curse was implanted inside an ancestor that has been passed along through the bloodline.

It always amazes me to hear how common witchcraft and voodoo are in this world. Many of those who live in poverty often have family members involved with dark forces. Many children are offered or dedicated to satanic principalities while still in utero. When studying these occult practices, one easily sees how twisted and maniacal the ceremonies are. Sadly, many animals and children are stolen and murdered for these ceremonies. These societies and covens often require blood sacrifices to their deity in exchange for more power. There is plenty of information about those sorts of rituals out there, all of which are centered on trading shed blood with unclean spirits for power. I would rather focus on the supreme power of Jesus, rather than the false sacrament of the demonic realm.

To share a personal experience about the very real reality of the occult, one time while hanging out with my friends back in high school I experienced something that freaked me out. It was after midnight and we were driving around our sleepy town with nothing to do. We wound up driving to a neighboring burg that has a state park set deep in the outskirts of the forest. We wandered up to the top of a hill and before we could even light a cigarette, we heard voices. There, looking over to the other side of the park where a tall obelisk monument stood commemorating dead soldiers of the revolutionary war, three torches were lit and a small group of people in hooded robes were running down the hill towards us. I could not believe my eyes. I wanted to know what they were doing and who they were. Looking back I saw my friends already hallway down the hill towards the car! Some friends! I took another look at the robed people carrying the torches. They were shouting as they rushed towards us. Quickly I turned and bolted towards the car.

Lots of people talked about occult activity in the area, and a nearby town has been known to be the witchcraft capital of the U.S. No, it is not Salem, Massachusetts. Many times growing up I heard stories of animal sacrifices in the woods near our home. Had we stumbled upon one of those cult sacrifices that night? I don't know.

We are going to talk more about witchcraft and curses relating to the blood in the coming chapters in order to break free from it. For now, know that while witchcraft in the bloodlines opens the door to curses, you have the right to cast curses out. Renounce those ties to witchcraft for yourself and your family line, repent, and ask for cleansing by the blood of Jesus. Every day I pray a quick and simple prayer when I take communion that you, too, should adopt. Say "In the name of Jesus, Lord I ask that you cleanse my DNA of any sickness, disease, curse, and impurity, all the way back to the generation of Adam, in Jesus name."

When taking communion, we should realize that it is not for the sole purpose of remembering the pain Jesus endured for us, although that is very important. The communion should be taken often as a way to align your DNA with the DNA of God. When you match the frequency of Jesus, your body begins to transform to what is in heaven. There are many teachings by Ian Clayton on the power of DNA cleansing and communion. I would urge you to seek these recordings and absorb the teachings many times. He illustrates the power of taking proper and regular communion (more than once a month!) better than I can. As you grow, you begin to understand principles and scripture much clearer. Always remember that Jesus was the ultimate blood sacrifice that atoned for our sins. Anything less is just a weak attempt to pervert what has already been finished by the power of God.

CHAPTER 4

PROCRASTINATION

It's all a faith walk. Plain and simple. Each and every single step is a movement towards what we trust is the right direction towards our Creator. I had been attending regular men's group meetings at a local church and really trying to press in and understand the Word more clearly. I wanted to understand more of these ancient mysteries and I needed a clearer picture of who God is, but I couldn't seem to find the answers I was looking for. This is very frustrating for a person like me because when I make my mind up about something, it is very hard for me not to accomplish my goal. It was already in my mind that I wanted a bigger picture of the Kingdom and I was not happy with hearing vague snippets from someone else's adventure. I wanted to experience these wild and miraculous stories for myself. It was no longer good enough to read about the heroes of faith in the bible. If these awesome things could happen 2,000 years ago, then they should be happening now, too!

The problem was that I had absolutely no grid or foundation whatsoever to receive what I was after. Raised in a private school up until the sixth grade, I learned to read the King James Version of the bible and was taught to not ask questions. I do not hold any offense to anyone from that time as I was only being taught a protocol that the teachers learned themselves. They were brought up just as I was.

Unfortunately, none of it seemed real to me. There was no explanation for simple theology. The logic of the school was to read and accept the New Testament in a language that seemed outdated and un-relatable. I was left in the dark as to why the Old Testament was even included. No one could provide answers because the message was simply "God used to be angry, then Jesus came, and now God loves you." That was how I perceived the school's logic. So when I spiraled out of control later in my life, my thought was "well at least God won't smite me because Jesus loves me, right?" The theory did not hold enough water for me to invest any energy into pursuing. Until I saw for myself his saving grace time and time again would I seek deliverance and hit the reset button on my life.

Early in 2014, I was invited to Moravian Falls in North Carolina for a glory conference. I was initially very excited and looking forward to the gathering. After all, it was another long winter in the northeast and a conference in May, still two months away, felt like a much-needed escape from the bitter New England weather. However, as May approached I began to change my tune and I began to let the stress of the trip overwhelm me. The thought of requesting time off from work from a busy kitchen, dealing with airplanes, and sitting in a room full of strangers for hours on end was starting to rack up. The idea of cancelling became even more appealing as I quickly reverted to what I believe to be one of the enemy's favorite words: "procrastination." I thought to myself, "there will be other conferences, I will just go to the next one."

The very week of the trip came and I had just about convinced myself to skip the powwow when a phrase that had been circulating rather frequently throughout the Christian community jumped out and really kicked me in the pants: "Step out of the comfort and into the courageous." What a great mantra! On the surface I thought that procrastination was comfortable. I figured it was putting important things off in order to make an excuse for lazy faith. Now, I think that it is the opposite. Not the lazy faith part; however, the comfort itself. When procrastinating something that is necessary, things just become more difficult. Just ask Jonah!

CROSS COUNTRY

It is always harder to run from God than to answer his call, as I found out through my own experience. Just look at our friend, Jonah. He runs away from the task that God has called him to do and ends in a very tight situation. One might think that running from a difficult job or putting off a necessary responsibility is easier than the discomfort and difficulty of facing the vocation. In the end, the situation can become volatile and much more intense than bargained for!

In the book of Jonah 1:10 it says that a violent storm erupted and "the men [on the ship] became extremely frightened and they said to him [Jonah], 'How could you do this?' For the men knew he was fleeing from the presence of the Lord, because he had told them." I think it's funny that even someone not focused on either running to or from God can recognize when someone else has a destiny. So then they said to him, "What should we do to you that the sea may become calm for us? For the sea was becoming increasingly stormy" (vs 11). This passage reminds me of what a friend of mine signs his e-mails with. He writes: "It's easier to just do the right thing the first time, rather than to make up excuses for why you didn't." This is so true. It takes great courage to step out of what is comfortable.

Many people ignore the callings placed on their lives because they are uncomfortable with the requirements. Many place assignments on hold. They put off what they know they are supposed to do because of fear, laziness, or even pride. I imagine the Lord is quite frustrated to constantly be let down by children who fight him and run away from their responsibilities, hoping that he forgets. But, as the scripture states, "...It is useless for you to fight against my will" (Acts 26:14, *NLT*).

Even more people are too afraid to do what is asked of them, while others are just lazy. Whatever the case, it's disobedience. Some start off strong but do not have the stamina to finish the same way. Some people allow sin to enter and take over their lives and knock them way off course. Often, people get angry because when they do obey the Lord they do not see immediate results and conclude that God made a mistake. And yet some others let pride blind them, thinking that their accomplishments were in direct relation to their own strength rather than God's.

Looking in 2 Chronicles 24:20, Zechariah tries to talk some sense into Joash. The passage begins with Zechariah asking why Joash is disobeying the Lord's commands. He goes on to say that because of this, Joash will not prosper. Joash is a man who started off like a real superstar. He rebuilt the Lord's temple only to then decide that he didn't need to listen to God anymore. How does that happen? Arrogance. Joash closed his ears to the Lord and was not only wounded in battle; but then while suffering from the damage, he was murdered in his bed. When one is disobedient, he opens himself up to the attacks of the enemy. Not only that, but ultimately, he will not prosper. Disobedience is a sin. As the Bible states, the law of sin is one that always leads to death.

UNSOLICITED CONFIRMATION

I did end up going to Moravian Falls and with the feeling of great anticipation. I knew that because I did not give in to the stress and curve balls leading up to the trip that something spectacular was waiting. It is one thing to read about the glory of God, and another thing to listen to a tape, or watch a DVD. However, it is *completely* different to witness it right before your eyes; to experience the power of his majesty first hand is overwhelming. The Christian circle I was a part of heard it all the time: signs and wonders, supernatural healings, angelic beings, and the manifestation of gold and precious stones, all happening in random churches around the world. To witness such things in a first hand account was truly a spectacular experience. I had only seen these sorts of miracles on DVD or videos on the computer. Up until that point, I had only heard about what seemed to be sensationalized fiction from the mythical narration of others. To actually see it was an awakening, which would be the best word I could use to articulate the sensation of being apart of the Kingdom Glory.

Though the meeting was held in a hotel conference area, I could feel the thickened atmosphere shifting in waves as the spirit of the Lord moved throughout the room. What I experienced was very much like what is written in Habakkuk 2:14, "For as the waters fill the sea, the earth will be filled with an awareness of the glory of the LORD" (*NLT*). That feeling comes from expectation. When we expect something, we get excited. That excitement causes a shift deep inside, and the spirit man is activated like a magnet.

I remember how each and every speaker got up and spoke about things and released words that my family and myself had been hearing in our prayer lives for a long time. The feeling of confirmation for me is part relief and part excitement. The electrifying feeling of knowing that everything that I thought I was hearing from the Creator was then paired with the comfort of knowing that I am not a crazy person. When one is in proper alignment with the Lord, he can receive those "downloads," as people like to often say, and receive them clearly! Hearing something in the quietness of one's spirit and then hearing it publically as unsolicited confirmation is an encouraging motivation to press in even more. It means one is just starting to scratch the surface.

Many people get confirmation and think "that's it, confirmation and done, I heard correctly." When one pushes farther, the ability to move expands beyond this dimension and cultivates a much more intimate relationship with the Creator. Had I ignored or procrastinated the calling I felt to go to North Carolina that week, you would not be reading this book. Let this be confirmation to you that nothing happens by chance.

There are no coincidences in life. The conference I attended in North Carolina was a divine appointment for me set forth as confirmation to release the message I was given to share. I believe that this book is only a tiny part of His perfect and pleasing will for my life. I believe in heavenly ordained appointments. I equate it to a job interview. One can do his research on a company. He can tailor his resume and get the call to come in and speak to the hiring manager. If he fails to show up, someone else will. If he does decide to show up, he still has to accept the job. There is always someone else who is willing to step into the role if he opts out.

God has set before you a job interview. Will you show up? Will you take the job? Make sure you are preparing yourself to answer the call. Be strong enough to step up to do whatever it is that you were created to do instead of withdrawing into the dry valley of regret. The floodgates are ready to burst open over your life in every way, both naturally, and supernaturally, but only if you are willing to walk out your destiny!

God rewards us with a tidal wave of favor when we accept the calling on our lives. A tsunami of favor and blessing is released when we are obedient to his request. The thing is, we have to quiet ourselves and tap into him. The Bible talks about a still small voice within each of us. We need to pay attention and trust that we are walking in proper alignment so that we can hear that voice clearly. The confirmation will be there for us every time we step out of our comfort zone and begin to walk in the courageous—although sometimes it may take some pressing in to receive.

Like I said, it is all a faith walk. We do not get a certified letter in the mail with steps one through ten written out for us. There is no trust in that and there is no strengthening in that approach. God is much more creative and clever than that. He wants to build us up; that is how a person learns. We can read all the textbooks we want, but nothing can, or will, compare to on the job training. Fortunately, we have the master of eternity who is ruler of time and space as our teacher. His tutelage guides us through the unknown.

However, just because we accept the Lord as our personal savior and receive salvation through the precious blood of Jesus, does not mean we should stand by idly and let others do the heavy lifting. We all have specific jobs and roles that need to be walked out in order to advance the Kingdom here on earth. We are literally in the middle of a war zone of a fallen world where we are trusted to complete the missions we were assigned. God will never allow us to go up against something that we cannot overcome, yet often it involves stretching us to a level of discomfort. The jurisdiction of our authority grows as we proceed along a righteous path. Therefore, the levels at which we engage in battle also must increase.

The greater the victory, the greater the reward. These are places that those with lazy faith will never ever see. We have to be aware of the authority we walk in order to achieve strategic victory. I love Romans 12:6-8, which lays out very clearly a person's role in the Kingdom:

"We have different gifts, according to the grace given to us. If your gift is prophesying, then prophesy in accordance with your faith; if it is serving, then serve; if it is teaching, then teach; if it is to encourage, then give encouragement, if it is giving, then give generously; if it is to lead, then do it diligently; if it is to show mercy, do it cheerfully."

Each person has been given his own gift and his own calling for the workings of the greater purpose. An arm cannot do the job of a leg, and the heart cannot do the job of a liver. Many question their significance or their purpose in the kingdom of God, to which I would reply that although the brain weighs a very small percentage of a person's body weight, it carries out a great deal of the body's functions! But, it must first work to make an impact.

There are plenty of dilettantes who are quietly passing through life and going through the motions of being a Christian. Such are "Tourists in the Faith." These are the same people who many times complain that they do not see breakthrough. They wonder why God does not move on their behalf and why they do not see the change that they feel they deserve. Relationships take work, and the more one puts in, the more increase one experiences. God needs to know that he can trust us. Seeking him out involves much more than punching the time card on Sunday mornings. We cannot just show up and play church for an hour and expect the mountains in our lives to move. God has not called us to be a social club and keep Him out of the clique.

I have seen bumper stickers and tee shirts that are marked with "It's a relationship, not a religion." This is true, and part of what Paul is talking about in 2 Timothy 2:15 clearly illustrates the fact that we are to put in real time with our relationship. Building reliance involves lots of examination in personal quiet time. Such reflection and prayer leads to greater understanding and is what is meant by the passage exhorting the Christian to "Study to show thyself approved unto God, a workman that needeth not to be ashamed, rightly dividing the word of truth" (*KJV*). If many Christians treated their friends the way they treat God, they would really be in trouble.

God does not accept phoning it in. When someone hires a contractor to do work on a house, they need to look up reviews on the internet and take all accounts into consideration. Falling victim to a silver tongued swindler who promises the most beautiful kitchen in half the time for less is easier than one would think! God does his research and knows who is willing to pick up the torch and be the light. He wants a professional to do the work right. Let God know you are serious about stepping into the place that he has called you to be in so that you can position yourself for success. An awareness and understanding of what is written in the Bible is what allows us to speak and act with authority, but it is the relationship that shows ourselves approved.

Growing up in the private school gave me a foundation of knowing about God. It was when I stepped out and decided I wanted a real relationship with him that I started to know him. Building a one-on-one relationship with God is what allows him to trust you more with the plans he has for you to succeed. There is a world of difference between the casual Christian, and the radical one. God is way more than what any of us have been taught. In order to accomplish what you have pre-ordained to do, you must put forth an effort to know not only who you are, but who He is. It is then that you can stop stalling your calling and walk out the fullness of your destiny.

CHAPTER 5

LINEAGE

Sometimes we act out our roles without thinking. There are select groups of people who know right away from a young age what they want to do with their life. They have the checklists all written out and they start to knock each line off one by one. Those are the people we don't like! Of course I am just kidding, but for the rest of us, it takes time to cultivate and learn what our true passions are. Sometimes they change and sometimes we never even discover what our gifts are really meant for. How sad is it to waste something that can only be performed by you?

My brother Erik knew what he wanted to do with his life. It just took a little time for him to make the right connections and learn what he needed to do in order to start walking out the dream he had in his heart. If it were up to him, Erik would have been involved as a wrestling promoter when he was ten years old! That was not part of God's timeline, though. Erik was patient while he walked out his scroll for this earth.

Erik was unique in that he was willing to hear and obey God in the steps he needed to take to carry out his calling.

Though he did not always trust his own instincts, his willingness proved to be an important factor in fulfilling his destiny. Had he deviated from the set timeline and done things out of his own logic and intent, important steps would be missing for his foundation. He was a good steward of his gifts and exercised his talents to a point of great strength. Such is the strength needed to achieve radical success. Erik did not live a long time here on this earth, but in his life he accomplished more than those who live twice as long. To live out one's calling requires willingness and obedience to live unconventionally—something Erik did quite well and is an inspiration for my own life.

We all have a natural inheritance of gifts and talents that are passed down from our parents and grandparents. For much of my life I never understood why we only excel in certain areas like mathematics or painting, and yet be terrible at writing or athletics. These talents and learning capabilities are usually a balance of things passed down from both parental lines. It was also unclear to me why specific interests and developments seem to skip generations. For example, a grandparent and grandchild have a predisposition towards art while the middle generation is quite the opposite. My thought was that if someone in my family had a knack or talent for something, then why could I not have that same strength? What then is the purpose of continuing just a last name?

Families meld with other families and produce offspring that takes on certain traits, only to pass combinations of these gifts down through the lineage. I feel that if we were in fact the evolutionary creatures that many people think we are, why would we stop at the point where we have come to and limit the potential of our capabilities? Should we not be progressing towards an evolved superhuman with both intelligence and skillset? Why would we cap ourselves with boundaries? If gifts and talents exist inside of us at this very moment, why can we not access them so that when we procreate, our children are in fact starting in a better place than we did? Further, if we are made up of a double strand of DNA from our mother and father, then should we not be able to align ourselves with a third cord of DNA—the blood of Jesus?

These are the kind of things I think about.

There has to be a connection between the strands of genetics that we come from, and the purpose we have in walking this earth. I do not believe in random chance. I do not believe the perfection of Gods pleasing will can allow coincidence to play any part. The gifts and talents we each possess come from a place that is pre-determined. Part of our walk, I believe is to understand what parts, or parts of our lineage need to be activated in order for us to achieve what we have been called here to do.

ORIGIN STORY

I remember the first time I ever read the Bible all the way through. One thing I noticed was that in one section, there were chapters after chapters of lists. To me, it was nothing more than a boring progressive march of names. "So and so begat so and so," and then that "so and so" begat another "so and so." List after list after list of all these names! There was a time when I was a kid that I honestly thought that the reason we were not taught the Old Testament in school was because it was comprised of so many lists, that the books were nothing more than an ancient census. Why these lists carried such importance never made much sense to me. For years I wondered why this was, and ironically the answer came when I just stopped overthinking things and asked God.

Before I explain, let me just back up a moment. First of all, the word "list" is defined as "a number of connected items or names written or printed consecutively, typically one below the other." The key word here is being *connected*. We are here based on a consecutive connection: our lineage.

The Bible hammers home the importance of our lineage over and over in these lists, as well as in many other stories and parables. The very thing connecting us to our lineage is much more than a common surname; it is the blood, a permanent irrefutable link to the past. Blood consists of a manuscript of connections all the way down to the quantum levels of vibration. The quantum level is the same level where the Creator breathed life into us. In the blood lay the recordings of our creation and the substance of blood carries its own frequency. DNA strands are literally scrolls that, once unraveled, read each and every gift and trait that is found within one's family bloodline. In essence, every gift that our ancestors received from the Creator is recorded within our DNA and is accessible within us right now!

I believe we have legal access to these locked treasures based on what is best articulated with the word "inheritance." An inheritance is received through historic and genealogical recording. In other words, they are received through lists. Second Chronicles 31 contains the answer that

I had been searching out in regards to the importance of lists. After many genealogic and historical records, the key to understanding them lies in the actions taken by Hezekiah after Passover. Glazing over the lists often causes one to neglect reading into what happens *after* the lists.

• • •

"When all this had ended, the Israelites who were there went out to the towns of Judah, smashed the sacred stones and cut down the Asherah poles. They destroyed the high places and the alters throughout Judah and Benjamin and in Ephraim and Manasseh. After they had destroyed all of them, the Israelites returned to their own towns and to their own property.

Hezekiah assigned the priests and Levites to divisions-each of them according to their own duties as priests or Levites-to offer burnt offerings and fellowship offerings, to minister, to give thanks and to sing praises at the gates of the Lord's dwelling. The king contributed from his own possessions for the morning and evening burnt offerings and for the burnt offerings on the Sabbath, at the New Moons and at the appointed festivals as written in the Law of the Lord. He ordered the people living in Jerusalem to give the portion due the priests and Levites so they could devote themselves to the Law of the Lord. As soon as the order went out, the Israelites generously gave the first fruits of their grain, new wine, olive oil and honey and all that the fields produced. They brought a great amount a tithe of everything. The People of Israel and Judah who also lived in the towns of Judah also brought a tithe of their herds and flocks and a tithe of the holy things dedicated to the Lord their God, and they piled them in heaps.

They began doing this in the third month and finished in the seventh month. When Hezekiah and his officials came and saw the heaps, they praised the Lord and blessed his people Israel.

Hezekiah asked the priests and Levites about the heaps; and Azariah the chief priest, from the family of Zadok, answered, "since the people began to bring their contributions to the temple of the Lord, we have had enough to eat and plenty to spare, because the Lord has blessed his people, and this great amount is left over."

Hezekiah gave orders to prepare storerooms in the temple of the Lord, and this was done. Then they faithfully brought in the contributions, tithes and dedicated gifts. Konaniah, a Levite, was the overseer in charge of these things, and his brother Shimei was next in rank. Jehial, Azaziah, Nahath, Asahel, Jerimoth, Jozabad, Eliel, Ishmakiah, Mahath, and Benaiah were assistants of Konaniah and Shimei his brother. All these served by appointment of King Hezekiah and Azariah the official in charge of the temple of God.

Kore son of Imnah the Levite, keeper of the East Gate, was in charge of the freewill offerings given to God, distributing the contributions made to the Lord and also the consecrated gifts. Eden, Miniamin, Jeshua, Shemaiah, Amariah, and Shekenaiah, assisted him faithfully in the towns of the priests, distributing to their fellow priests according to their divisions, old and young alike.

In addition, they distributed to the males three years old or more whose names were in the genealogical records-all who would enter the temple of the Lord to perform the daily duties and various tasks, according to their responsibilities and their divisions. And they distributed to the priests enrolled by their *families in the genealogical records and likewise to the Levites twenty years old or more, according to their responsibilities and their divisions. They included all the little ones, the wives, and the sons and daughters of the whole community listed in these genealogical records. For they were faithful in consecrating themselves.*

As for the priests, the descendants of Aron, who lived on the farmlands around their towns or in any other towns, men were designated by name to distribute portions to every male amongst them and to all who were recorded in the genealogies of the Levites.

This is what Hezekiah did throughout Judah, doing what was good and right and faithful before the Lord his God. In everything that he undertook in the service of God's temple and in obedience to the law and the commands, he sought his God and worked wholeheartedly. And so he prospered." (NIV).

• • •

This particular chapter is often used to teach on tithing—which is not inaccurate, especially if you want to be bound by that law. However, peeling back the layers reveals so much more. The importance of cleansing the genealogy is exhibited figuratively in the cleansing of the Israelite land. Early in the chapter that which was considered unclean was destroyed, including unholy altars, Asherah poles, and idols. After this cleansing the Israelites returned to their homes and property with a reformation and realignment. The connection between the genealogy and cleansing land has strong connections based on the context of Chronicles.

Looking a bit deeper into the beginning of chapter 31,

what is found is that before a person can change, cleansing needs to take place. Think about this: when a doctor sees a patient one of the first questions asked is whether the patient has a certain family history of specific conditions. Often when a person who experiences cancers and disease, the sickness can be linked to someone else within the previous generations of their lineage. This is commonly known as a generational curse. In order to be free from these curses cleansing must take place.

Much like there are generational curses, there are blessings hidden in the genetic code as well. The writer of Chronicles describes how good works "pile up" in "heaps." These good works are so much that there are storehouses erected and guarded to steward the abundance. The text goes on to explain that first fruits and new wine are to be distributed to the people based on genealogical records. In other words, these storehouses are so full and are distributed when proof from lineage is shown. Unfortunately, many of these storehouses go untapped because no one in the bloodline has learned to access them.

Hosea explicitly states in verse 4:6 that people are "destroyed" for their lack of knowledge. By neglecting our duties to press in and learn the secret ways of the Lord, why then should he trust us with the sacred knowledge that comes with building a deep friendship with him?

The author of Chronicles understood this gives a step-by-step guide to aid us in prosperity. Hidden in 2 Chronicles 31:20-21 is a four-part guide to unlocking that which is already laid up for us waiting to be claimed. Those four parts are comprised of the following list:

1. Have faith in God
2. Obey God's laws and commands
3. Seek God
4. Work wholeheartedly

The last step is one that I enjoy especially. To be a Christian does not mean one can be lukewarm; he is either in or out. Living the life of a Christian is not for the lazy.

I have heard for years to expect the wealth of the wicked, to expect change to just happen, and to look for provision. Expectation is absolutely necessary to step into the excitement of that reality. On the other hand, thinking that the wealth of the wicked is going to show in the form of some out of state second party paycheck will result in some sour news—don't hold your breath!

Seeing that which has been promised of prosperity and the blessings hidden in our bloodlines requires putting in the effort to seeking God. Our generations have been storing up riches in the supernatural reality and we are entitled to them, but the unclaimed "heaps" are accessible through a trek and a journey that demands a certain level of spiritual fitness. Just like climbing a natural mountain, it takes dedication and preparation to reach the goal.

The scriptures are so clear in that they describe blessings being dispersed through genealogical records. Such gifts and traits are the multipliers that make a person go beyond his or her current capabilities.

It actually reminds me of pinball. I love playing pinball because of the sensory overload and experience, including the lights, sounds, and competition. At first it seems impossible to achieve the high scores on the rankings list. Yet after taking some time to read the tiny little rule card on the machine, how to succeed becomes very clear. Most people do not even realize that every machine has a set of rules just below the play field! Learning to play the game correctly results in maximizing the full enjoyment of the game.

Each pinball game is full of score multipliers and super multipliers. Some even have mega multipliers. Hitting specific skill shots and playing the rules of the game will cause a player to achieve high scores. Instead of just aimlessly pressing the flippers and hoping to keep the silver ball from dropping out of the playing field, learning how to play and keeping within the guidelines adds meaning and strategy to the game. But, playing by the rules is not enough—playing it safe and not shooting the skill shots will never get the score on the scoreboard! Hitting the multipliers and super multipliers are necessary in winning the game.

Just like pinball, understanding the rules allows us the opportunity to stack up the multipliers (gifts and talents) within us that are waiting to be claimed. Talk about a super jackpot!

Too many people only look at things with a mindset of not dropping the ball. They have high hopes but only put in minimal effort so they do not lose. Such thinking needs to be reversed and those people need to break away from that archaic approach. God is bigger than any defeat in our lives. We need to stop trying so hard not to lose, and instead begin to think about how much we can achieve through him. We have a responsibility and a purpose that does not include losing.

Looking again at 2 Chronicles 31, people are not only receiving their rightful inheritances, but they are also being delegated tasks and endowed with responsibilities. Offerings and sacrifices are also taking place. People are consecrating themselves for the purpose of their existence. The amount of information laid out in this chapter is wild!

One line in particular holds great significance and skipping over it negates the weight of the entire chapter. Verse 3 states "The King gave offerings and made sacrifices on the Sabbath, new moons, and the appointed festivals as written in the law of the Lord" (*NIV*). Breaking off the grid of this mindset is key. We need to begin to transition our thanksgiving unto God based on when his law states. We are spirit beings, although we are housed inside a body made of flesh, and we should not adhere to the governing system of manufactured tradition and giving. Distancing ourselves from when the mall or warehouse store dictate celebration is critical to seeing change in our lives. Corporations do a great job of marketing during "holidays," be it Valentine's Day, Christmas, Easter, and more. Each of these is a manufactured tradition set by profit driven companies. News flash: Baby Jesus was not born a week before the ball dropped in Times Square. This is a strategy put into place long ago to get God's children off course and to rob them of their rightful inheritance that they can be cashing in on all year 'round!

We talked earlier about the false grid of time. One of the ways we allow ourselves to be enslaved by this imaginary grid is by being distracted by manufactured holidays. Many of the "Christian Festivals" are nothing more than corporate agendas that are designed for profit. Getting away from the distractions and false doctrines of celebrating and giving is all well and good, but there is still one major thing we as believers need to do in order to position ourselves to unlock our God given birthright. This is the matter of the blood. We spoke about the importance of it earlier and now we are about to take a look at taking to task our corrupted DNA.

SPRING CLEANING

Cleansing is one of the most important ways that a person can begin to alter the expression of his or her DNA. In order to do this, one needs to make the conscious effort to press in and repent to activate all that is available to him. Just as the blood scrolls record the gifts and talents given by the Creator, it also records the adverse effects of living in a fallen world. Fortunately, words have power. By speaking to the baseline makeup with the authority given by Christ, one can start to purify his or herself to a point where they can receive what is waiting.

To do so requires simply coming before God in the name of his son Jesus, through faith. Visualize the movement, and action of pushing through the plasma membrane of the body. Envision moving past the cellular walls, deeper and deeper where the atoms of the body resonate. It sounds very strange to people at first, but the imagination is the most creative gateway we have that allows us access into the supernatural realms.

Our minds are heavenly microscopes, which have optics and lenses that multiply even past existing imaginative theories of consciousness. This sounds really far out, even borderline ridiculous. We have to move past that denial and insecurity of what we believe to be logical thinking. Logical thinking can be (and often is) a hindrance when trying to move into supernatural thinking. The "voice of reason" is part of the problem because it has been battered and twisted for so long that we think we cannot possibly do or see the impossible without explanation.

We cannot rationalize something that is beyond understanding. We need to put our faith in where God is leading us and have the expectation of visualization. Deep inside the quantum mechanics of our mind, past the electrical currents and charged atoms, we enter the immeasurable quark levels from which sub atomic particles are made up of. There is an infinite space between the multiples of action and movement called the Planck-constant. Go deeper! I can rattle off these generic scientific terms and definitions all day, but the fact of the matter is, is that we have to choose to let our spirit overtake our stubborn brain and follow the course to wherever God brings us.

It is not about compound scientific theories that have been postulated and dissected by varying levels of scientific genius. Rather, it is about listening to the still small voice that cannot be captured anywhere but within our own being. Ask God to cleanse and disinfect what is filthy and unclean. Ask Him to sterilize and sanitize your blood. Ask Him to restore and realign the very recording he made of your existence. Thank him for the complete forgiveness of sin that has been carried through each generation in your lineage all the way back to Adam and begin to see your life change.

CHAPTER 6

IMPARTATION

One by one, heavenly beings manifested in front of my eyes as if I was squinting at a mirage and trying to understand the possibility of what I was seeing. These beings were basking in the glory of the Lord just like we were. The anointing on the musicians was outstanding and opened up the atmosphere so that we as participants could be perceptive to what was happening in the spirit realm. I remember being at the conference in North Carolina and seeing so clearly into the supernatural. To see things with the natural eye for more than a flash or quick second was pretty incredible, putting it mildly.

In awe, I sat in my chair and gazed at the entities. They seemed to be everywhere. The podium was flanked with what looked like an open portal. No longer was a wall standing behind the instruments, but a vast cascading wall of rejoicing angels. Rows of these beings stretched on for what seemed like an eternity off into the horizon. Never had I seen anything like it.

Open visions and sights are unlike anything the natural

eye can process. They leave a person with such an experience that can never be replaced with manufactured substances again. Sensing in the body pales in comparison to the sensation of being in alignment with the spirit. Those who have ever had a heavenly encounter know this to be true and often these experiences become life changing.

Prior to this particular experience, I had these types of encounters many times. As a child it was very common for me to see angels and heavenly beings. Sometimes I would wake up in the middle of the night in the house I grew up in and see a large angel standing watch. He had a tall spear, a big shield, and giant wings; although, I could never perceive its entire body because it was nearly transparent. The angel always appeared to be outlines of moving silver. These shiny silver lines seemed to move like water in a constant state of motion even though the being stood motionless on guard. Talk about feeling protection!

The first time I saw the being, I woke up my brother and made him check it out to make sure I was not crazy. After a while I got used to the fact that there was something so intense protecting me as I slept and it became quite comforting. Even to this day I am aware of the beings. When I sense they are close I hold my hand up and say "high five." One day I expect to feel the high five being reciprocated and I will need to change my shorts.

• • •

The glory of God's presence was very thick in the conference atmosphere. The air in the room was almost damp, as I perceived a dewy mist settling on my nose. An unnatural brightness caused me to close my eyes at one point. In my spirit I saw yellow and gold ribbons fluttering and rippling across the canvas in my head. Entire legions of featureless faces were in front of me coming through the ribbons and rotated in a circular pattern. I did not understand what I was seeing and when I tried looking beyond the faces, a giant bear appeared and roar loudly. This bear was not threatening or violent towards me, although it almost felt like it was there to sound a war cry of some sort. Its razor sharp teeth were intimidating, yet instinctively I knew that this creature was not after me. Things like this seen in the spirit do not make sense logically but make perfect sense in the spirit.

When going to events like this, often the service will culminate with the prophet praying an impartation over those willing to receive it. An impartation is a way to receive an anointing. Romans 1:11-12 "For I long to see you, that I may impart to you some spiritual gift, so that you may be established- that is, that I may be encouraged together with you by the mutual faith both of you and me" (NKJV). This service was no different; however, the speaker emphasized that he was not the one with the power. Instead, the Spirit of God working through him is the source and therefore it was unnecessary to lay hands on people. We as believers have the opportunity to receive by faith since there is no distance in the spirit realm.

This same speaker instructed us that if we wanted an impartation, it was up to us to reach up and just pull it down. After days of seeing the supernatural right in front of me, I needed no convincing that the power of the Lord was much more than someone laying their hand on my head and praying. While the person speaking carried the message, it was my job to receive it and receive from the open heaven that was created in that atmosphere.

No longer was receiving on my part dependent on someone else making a motion and saying they have given me an invisible supernatural ability. Rather, it was a realization that God is much more than some mystery being who wants to only be worshipped. He is a God who is more than willing to give, yet wants us to trust him enough so that he can trust us back with the gifts he has for those who seek him. If I wanted more of him, my prerogative is to reach up and take it.

Where is the trust in someone who has what I was after just handing it over to me? It would be too easy for me to show up and collect a prize—that is lazy! I made up my mind that I wanted to delve deeper into my relationship with him. If that meant reaching up into thin air and grabbing at the ceiling tiles, I was going to do just that.

The very best example that comes to mind is the story of Elijah, and his servant Elisha. In 2 Kings we see a transference of anointing that gets doubled! Elijah is about to be taken away in a whirlwind. As Elijah makes his way towards the rendezvous, he tells his servant Elisha to stay put. Elisha refuses and continues his duty as servant to his master. Along the way, the townspeople taunt Elisha by telling him that his master is leaving him today. Elisha is not affected by their discouraging remarks and tells them the shut up. Just before Elijah is taken away, he asks his servant Elisha what he can do for him as thanks for his loyal service. Elisha asks to inherit a double portion of Elijah's mantle, or anointing. Elijah tells his servant that although a difficult request, if he can see Elijah depart, the blessing will be his.

Elisha was stubborn (in a good way) and refused to leave his masters side. He even rose above the antagonistic, and discouraging banter of the townsfolk and remained focused on his role. When Elijah told his servant that it was a difficult request-but if Elisha saw it, he would inherit the double anointing- it was up to Elisha to receive. Elijah didn't just fork it over. The inheritance Elisha asked for became less than Elijah's willingness to give it, but rather more of Elisha's job to receive it.

THE FLYING JAWBONE

My forearms felt like they were going to explode! As I was reaching up into the glory cloud above my head and pulling straight down, my muscles throbbed and threatened to tear through my blazer. It was like Dr. Bruce Banner changing into the Incredible Hulk, although I'm sure it only looked that spectacular in my own mind! As I relaxed my arms from pulling felt as though I was going to pass out from exhausting all the strength in my upper body.

In my mind I saw a reddish-orange glowing jawbone with lines of heat behind it. When I opened my eyes, the bone was hovering above my head and consumed in a golden fire. As I pulled the jawbone down I fell back into my chair and immediately a voice thundered the phrase "Time to slay the Philistines!" Whether the voice was audible in my ears or in my spirit I do not know.

I shook my hands a bit because they felt as if they too had been set on fire. The prickly pressure surged throughout my entire body as I sat in my chair coming down from an incredible spiritual high. Though this jawbone was in a different realm than the physical, I had spent all of my energy to pull it into the physical realm by faith. Eventually the fatigue ended and before I knew it the conference was over. That night in the hotel room I showered and crawled into bed, my mind racing with images of golden fire and red jawbones.

I lay in bed disappointed that the evening was over and contemplated going back downstairs to the conference hall just to see if I could soak up anymore of the supernatural atmosphere I had experienced the past few days. Many things were going through my mind when my cell phone sounded. I reluctantly got up to check the notification to see who would be pestering me at such a late hour. My sister, Jenna, of course.

She had been at the conference as well, and had been up thinking about everything just as I was, only a few doors down. Remembering something that our aunt had told us about several years prior, she began doing research almost immediately upon entering her hotel room in regards to some of the impartations and revelation that had been given during that final session. I read her text and her message was startling enough that if I had any intentions of sleeping, those thoughts went out the window as I spent the rest of the night trying to connect invisible dots even further.

TATTOO YOU

The message I received from my sister Jenna was brief but exciting. Somewhere between all of the topics discussed at the last session, including a brief stint about being able to collect generational gifts, a light bulb went off as she remembered that we were related to Sir Isaac Newton. Not just distantly, but direct descendants. A quick Google search resulted in discovering a college in Massachusetts only a few hours from our home that housed many of Sir Isaac Newton's possessions. Some of the items in the collection included manuscripts and the entire fore-parlor from his home in England. The dots began to connect.

All night I sat thinking about what our relation could mean from a spiritual standpoint. The pondering continued through the next day. Sitting in an airport waiting to board a flight to New York, I casually glanced down at my left forearm. I gasped as I realized why my left forearm was burning so bad during the impartation the night before! There on my forearm I have a tattoo of the Newton family Crest. How could I forget? Anyone who has had a tattoo for a long time can attest to forgetting they are inked. It just becomes a part of the self, and often one forgets he or she even has it. So, when I glanced down and saw the fading ink of the Newton family shield, things began to click and my spirit lit back up.

"We have to go to Boston!" I practically shouted out loud in my "a-ha!" moment.

My arm was reacting like a metal detector, and I sensed strongly a treasure laid hidden for us at this college in Massachusetts. Further research confirmed that we are in fact related to Sir Isaac Newton—one of the greatest minds in all of science history. Though not directly in the sense that he bore no children, but in that through the bloodlines we are as direct as possible through his father's brother.

Sir Isaac Newton was a pioneer in the scientific revolution. Many people think of him and recall the story of how an apple supposedly fell on his head, thus leading to the discovery of gravity. Newton's genius intellect reached far beyond this contribution to the scientific community. Interestingly, Newton was a Christian whom devoted much of his life to the study of ancient biblical scripture and prophecy. It was his belief that he was, amongst others, part of a very small group of people chosen by God to interpret the bible accurately. We will talk about that small percentage later on.

So much of what we read in today's Bible has been translated from Hebrew to Greek, and from Greek to just about every modern language. Much of the original text has been interpreted in different ways due to multiple meanings attributed to each of the Hebrew words. Newton was able to learn and understand the Hebrew language so well that he translated the scripture in such a way that he emphasized the presence of multiple layers beyond the text at face value.

Many of us have heard of the "Bible code," where words are plugged into a computer program and specific word webs are generated in the results. These matrixes link words and phrases in clusters in different chapters of the bible. Such practice, however, is random and subject to chance occurrence. Newton was the first to see beyond just chance occurrence. He was convinced that the scriptures were in fact blueprints and instructions for something much greater. In fact, he was even quoted as saying "A few scattered persons which God hath chosen... can set themselves sincerely, and honesty to search after truth" (Yahuda manuscript). His extensive research in certain books of the bible included, but was not limited to, the book of Daniel and the book of Revelations.

His belief in discovering ancient secrets drew him to the eschatological books specifically because of the amount of prophetic text that is written in them. Additionally, Newton spent much of his life recreating diagrams and blueprints of King Solomon's Temple. Within the written description given in the ancient texts of the temple, Newton searched for mathematical coding and answers to his quest for a deeper understanding.

My theory suggests Newton operated under a very similar anointing, if not the same, as King Solomon. Both were incredibly intelligent men who had influence and authority over the natural world. Their knowledge of many subjects superseded that of anyone else in their lifetime. Also interesting to note is that King Solomon was the son of King David, a shepherd son of the farmer Jesse. Newton was the son of a farmer as well, yet despite the fact that neither were of noble birth, both men achieved a royal status in ruling kingdoms on earth.

Newton was knighted despite the lack of a royal birth— very rare unless his family was of great wealth in that era. In fact, he was not only knighted, but Newton was also put in charge as "Warden and Master" over the Royal Crowns mint. He governed the ministry of coins, and was the man responsible for changing the currency from the silver standard over to the gold standard. Like Newton, Solomon received divine wealth from God; so much so, that the silver in Solomon's time was worthless and gold became the new standard. Both men share many similarities yet lived many centuries—and many miles—apart.

Perhaps what connected them was that particular mantle, or anointing. Does that sound impossible to you? Consider this, we as a human race allow ourselves to be confined by rules and limitations in order to understand what we cannot explain. When you make the decisions to break free from the proverbial box that we quarantine ourselves in, we begin to see the possibilities beyond the walls placed in front of our faces. There is more than just a three dimensional reality!

Science has discovered that humanity lives in a world of three-dimensional holograms, and restrictions. When operating in the supernatural heavenly levels, the natural world has no choice but to bend and give way to the authority that we walk in. It must comply with the decrees of our King. Newton was distinguished with the opportunity and prestige normally reserved for those born into the circumstance, yet even he believed in the secrets hidden throughout the supernatural dimension. He devoted much of his life to diligent study of scripture and pressed in, developing and deep and intimate relationship with the Lord within a heavenly kingdom. This relationship that he cultivated inevitably manifested in the natural world he lived in by granting him the honor and prestige as the son a king. It stands as a clear testament of what was on Earth manifesting as it is in Heaven for Newton.

There is no way to know if Newton was a direct descendent of King Solomon, However, I believe we can come to the definitive conclusion that when you devote yourself to understanding ancient mysteries, your strengths develop in such a way that allow a person to take on more responsibility in the Kingdom. One not only moves in ancient biblical anointing's, but ultimately has the capacity to grow beyond anything that had been achieved thus far. I am motivated to go beyond the limitations that have been taught. We need to be proactive in our walk and take a progressive approach to understanding what has yet to be learned. I am no longer happy with being corralled into a box of lazy doctrine for the sake of convenience. I believe that profound experiences follow radical commitment. I intend on furthering my understanding of God's mysteries by building off of the foundation of wisdom found in scripture.

ALCHE-MYSTERY

I was fascinated to learn that Sir Isaac Newton believed that ancient and biblical wisdom was not only stored within sources in the Bible, but also in artifacts. That may sound far out to imagine; however, quite fitting to remember is that Newton was the same scientist that discovered the Law of Conservation of Energy. This law states that energy cannot be created nor uncreated, but can change from one form to another. Also fitting to remember is that Newton was a brilliant man who spent years and years just studying King Solomon's *temple*.

The temple in particular carried a great deal of significance to Newton. His theory suggested an underlying reason why Israelites not only regarded the temple as sacred, but also the ritual artifacts inside. His thought reasoned that within these vessels used in ritual ceremonies carried a portion of the wisdom and knowledge the Bible exhorts us to seek out. Ezra 6:5 talks about the inviolability of temple artifacts:

> "And also let the golden and silver vessels of
> the house of God, which Nebuchadnezzar
> took forth out of the temple which is at
> Jerusalem, and brought unto Babylon, be
> restored, and brought again unto the temple
> which is at Jerusalem, every one to his place,
> and place them in the house of God."(KJV)

Newton hypothesized that even metals possessed life. If seemingly inanimate objects can possess traces of life, then they have some sort of DNA or RNA. Or, at the very least, different nucleotides used to build a particular structure stable enough to have the ability to store sequential information in the molecules. Boring! Basically if there is life, then it has a recording of its creation just like we do.

Newton's interest in Alchemy notably contributed to the beginning of what is known today—and dreaded by many high school students—as Chemistry. Many alchemists before and after Newton's time have been intrigued with the idea of transforming metals into gold. Whether or not Newton was successful in that regard remains a mystery; however, in today's advanced movements in the glory, I myself have witnessed solid gold crowns of human teeth manifest inside of people's mouths right in front of my eyes. Such are miracles, signs, and wonders constantly boasted about, but many never experience.

Perhaps as the reader, you may balk at this experience. Before you grab the torch and pitchfork, first ask yourself why you may not have experienced these things. Do you believe in the possibility of gold teeth appearing in mouths? Do you believe that it is possible for science to manipulate matter in a lab, but not God manipulating matter in a church service? If God created light can he not create teeth?

Remember that whom we choose to follow in our walk needs to be producing good fruit. When we attend church or Christian conferences, we are listening to what God has done in that particular pastor or speaker's life. We listen to the experiences and beliefs in their walk and perhaps, if we are especially impressed, choose to seek the Lord in those particular areas. In doing so, we position ourselves to advance only up to the point of that particular leader's limitations. Church is a wonderful thing, but we need to remember to grow outside the church. A goldfish will only grow as large as its tank. Sometimes we need to step out of the four walls and into the limitless expanse of Christ and His word so that we can grow without boundary.

While in North Carolina, I had the opportunity to listen to Dr. Peter Wagner speak about the "Kingdom Ladder." If you have not heard of him, I would encourage you to research him and listen to the amazing amount of knowledge and understanding he beholds. In a nutshell, a three-step staircase illustrates the Kingdom Ladder. The first step is where the largest percent of believers are positioned: the focus on one's self and gaining a solid spiritual foundation. The second step is the focus on the church itself. This houses a smaller percent of people and includes pastors, musicians, volunteers, etc. These aid those who are on step one. The third step is the tiniest residency on the Ladder. Such people are the few who focus their efforts on the entire Kingdom and have a greater vision of Christ moving everywhere. Many people are content with sitting on the first step, and never going beyond a Sunday sermon. Should you be one of those persons, I would encourage you to continue walking up the flight of stairs into new levels of the Kingdom.

Wagner also has some interesting insight on what he considers is the Apostolic Structure. This structure is one of accountability where apostles are aligned with other apostles. The apostolic center focuses on all three steps of the Kingdom Ladder, whereas the majority of local churches will only focus on the first two, resulting in only limited growth. Take a look around you and determine if you are in the right place, and if not, determine whether you want to start your ascent up the ladder.

A friend of mine and guest on my show, prophetic evangelist Eddie T, once said that he lives an adventure every single day doing the work for his "Daddy." He says radical trust gives him radical favor. We are either in or out, no middle ground exists. If you are in, then you are no doubt going to be apart of the miraculous testimonies that are happening everyday! When seeing these things happen, the perception of reality shifts and understanding fragments of the Lord's capabilities begins to occur.

One of my favorite scriptures is in the book of Romans 12:1-2:

> "Therefore, I urge you, brothers and sisters, in view of God's mercy, to offer your bodies as a living sacrifice, holy and pleasing to God- this is your true and proper worship. Do not conform to the pattern of this world, but be transformed by the renewing power of your

mind. Then you will be able to test and approve what God's will is- his good, pleasing and perfect will" (NIV)

When I read that, I instantly connected to what the Apostle Paul was saying: turn from sin and change your thinking. The way many of us perceive and try to understand things is incorrect. Most of us are just not geniuses. Some of us even spell that word with a "J". We do things a certain way for so long and wonder why the result is not what we had hoped. Such approach is flawed. People like Sir Isaac Newton, Nikola Tesla, and Albert Einstein did not think like the majority. They were the smallest percent on the highest step. Not in a braggadocios way, but rather in a factual way that cannot be argued. I am encouraged to not only be on that level, but to move beyond it!

I understand that like contending for an invisible jawbone, reaching for something that doesn't seem to exist in a physical world is difficult to make sense of. This is the point! If something is not making sense, then I believe it is the right place to begin. Stepping out of what is comfortable is the first step in finding what is necessary to move beyond self-imposed limitations. When we begin to challenge ourselves to grow in places that do not seem possible, we start to trust in God more and more. We move towards our true calling.

Living a righteous life is a constant endeavor that trades our inadequacies for more of God. Ephesians 4:1 says "...I urge you to live a life worthy of the calling you have received" (*NIV*). If you are not called to make scientific discoveries, no big deal. Know that you *are* called for something that is just as important. Tap into the secret place of knowing God and expand your mind to allow the necessary change in your life for Kingdom favor. Therein lies your destiny that can leave a monumental impact on the history of the world.

CHAPTER 7

INHERITANCE

I am just as excited writing this today as I was the day we learned what was waiting for us three hours north in Massachusetts. In a college library just outside of Boston was a room that housed the original wooden walls, floors, doors, and mantle of the fore-parlor belonging to Sir Isaac Newton. The room miraculously survived a fire that occurred in Newton's home in London, England. Among some of the surviving relics housed in this college from Newton's personal collection were manuscripts and papers he had written. How these pieces of history made their way to the United States has quite the interesting backstory.

The spark that set the fire of fascination began through discovering one of the surviving manuscripts written decades before by Newton, oddly titled with the same name as the founders' surname. The founders were amazed at the coincidence and became avid collectors of Newtonia, and left their college with an inheritance of one of the largest collections in the world. Pieces including original books, handwritten manuscripts, engravings, and artifacts are amongst the massive collection. After a fire in Newton's London home, the house and its remaining pieces were set to be destroyed until these same founders stepped up and purchased the surviving woodwork. They were able to acquire the room and imported it to the United States, creating the Newton Room for private use only.

After a few emails with the college, our family received radical favor and had a date set to visit the room and learn even more from the gracious staff. We found out that when Newton died, it was discovered that he ironically did not leave a will. Having no children of his own, the British Government stepped in and seized his estate in order to pay off its own debts to the Royal Mint. We discovered from our genealogy report that while Newton had no children of his own, nor did he have any brothers by his father's blood, we come directly from the bloodline of Newton's uncle and his father's brother. Since Isaac had no children and no next of kin through the Newton family line who claimed his inheritance, we as family had claim to this estate based on the genealogical and historical records. Coincidence? I think not.

I believe that the inheritance left by Sir Isaac Newton still exists and expands far beyond a pile of papers and antique wood. Although it has been almost three hundred years, the anointing and gifts of the Spirit still remain. They are beyond time. The ageless and eternal power found in Christ never ends. In the natural, manuscripts and material possessions are better suited to remain in museums and under the care of curators and historians. They are not the inheritance that I am particularly interested in. However, the priceless inheritances that cannot be measured, bought, or stolen are in fact the true riches and are the ones that I am after. Though dormant, they can be awakened and taken further by continuing to uncover the secrets that are hidden within the supernatural realms.

The good news is that giant caches of abundance are stored up and waiting to be awakened in your life, also! They are the stored up "piles" and "heaps" from 2 Chronicles 31 that can push your position in the natural into the supernatural. These gifts propel you further beyond places where the great mysteries of the Lord are hidden. But first, it requires knowing what is yours in order to claim it legally. For example: the story of the Shunnamite woman in 2 Kings 8. The king restored all that belonged to her, as well as the income from the land from the day she had to leave, until now. For the Shunnamite woman, that was seven years. The income did not disappear, but rather it was restored by order of the King. The woman returned from the land of the philistines and prospered because of the legal rights she had. Her inheritance did not go away because she was not present to receive. It was waiting to be claimed—with interest!

I believe when I saw the jawbone, it was symbolic of the return of my family's inheritance as well as a victory over our enemies, much like Samson's infamous annihilation of the Philistines with only a jawbone. An inheritance is so much more than just a surname. It is an elegant composition of wisdom, gifts, and anointings. It just takes two very important things: The rightful heir to claim it and the appropriate level of maturity to move in them. I count close to three hundred years worth of income from the estate of Sir Isaac Newton that is owed! I have no doubt that my King will assign an official to this case and decree restoration just like he did when the Shunammite woman returned from the land of the Philistines.

Faith that things like this are possible is required to see what cannot be seen. Logic tells us that things like this are not possible. Those who align themselves with a God whose power is limited will not experience what is available to those who realize that God is bigger than human logic. Remember, He created us, not the other way around. What makes us think that we know more than he does? I choose to serve a God without limitations because of kingdom faith—a faith beyond my own puny restrictions. We need to put work into cleansing ourselves from the sin in our life as well as the transgressions from generations before us. We have to humble ourselves if we want to unlock the giant inheritance stored up in our bloodline. This is a requirement of faith beyond our own hope or imagination. We need to plug into the source and activate the kingdom faith. That is the first step in positioning ourselves to claim what is rightfully ours.

ANCESTOR STONE

I knew that I could not just waltz into the college and grab an anointing and split. I had an understanding of the weight of the situation. This was a very serious obligation to commit to. It was the beginning of a new and higher level of trust with God and I needed to dive into a deeper pursuit of his presence. In order to do that effectively, I first needed to quiet my mind and body in order to tap into a deep level of stillness. This journey began with a seven day fast. While in prayer I asked how long I should fast and I sensed that my answer lay within the Shunammite woman's story. Seven years' restoration jumped out at me. I sensed that God was impressing a seven-day fast was important and I committed to it wholeheartedly.

Fasting is a great way to break any unconfessed sin and allow the mind, body, and spirit to realign with God's Kingdom. Knowing that I needed direction and guidance in order to go about this the right way, I was determined to prevent any sin or transgression the ability to hinder and block me from grabbing my inheritance—in myself or in my bloodline. I truly believed that going to the Newton Room was a God ordained event. Because of this, I wanted the divine appointment to go as it was supposed to without any interference on my end.

I started the fast by hiking up to the highest point I knew of near my home. High atop a mountain in a state park I took in the scenery surrounding my lofty perch. I remember what a perfect spring evening it was. The green leaves of the tall oaks trees had finally bloomed as I made my way up to the top and found myself all alone. Despite the numerous cars and people wandering throughout the relatively busy park, I had the top of the mountain to myself. I took the time to pray and lay in the freshly trimmed grass under the early evening sky. It was a cloudless atmosphere, and the sky was incredibly blue.

In the stillness I visualized myself openly speaking to God and confessed my sins. I went before the courts and asked for forgiveness for the comprehensive list I had compiled of years of guilt. I also used the time to lay out my expectations and hopes, knowing that my time dwelling in the land of the Philistines was coming to end and that God was going to make all the wrongs right. I asked the Lord to guide me as walked into the unknown and stepped of the proverbial boat by faith. After all, as far as I knew, there was not a "how to" guide for this sort of thing. In my heart, I let him know that my trust was completely in Him.

This time on the mountain was a time of "divine correction." Prophetic evangelist Joshua Mills had recently spoke on this season at the conference I attended in North Carolina, and I had full expectation to see the three angels he spoke about released on the earth at that time. In his message, Joshua taught about the angels and their purpose. They were the angels "Reveal," "Realign," and "Restore." I remember hearing that and nearly fell off of my chair because it was such perfect timing. Everything God does is calculated and cerebral. With that said, I was fully expecting this angelic support as I stepped into this open door of inheritance.

On the mountain I asked God for some words to chew on during this fast. I sensed 1 John 5:14-15: "This is the confidence we have in approaching God: that if we ask anything according to his will, he hears us, And if we know that he hears us, whatever we ask, we know that we have what we asked of him" (NIV). I spent the week praying and trying to be still as I listened for instructions. During most of my free time I did little else but worshipped Him and prayed around the clock. I believed God would do his part and I wanted to make sure that I also did mine.

The night before we were to go to the college I sat down and asked God what to pray. I felt the need to write down what I was replaying over in my head. "There was an inheritance that was partly in slumber," I heard in my spirit, "as well as partly stolen in some measure." Proverbs 22:28

jumped out at me, in which people are warned not to take another person's birthright or claim. It says simply: "Don't remove an ancient boundary stone that was set up by your ancestors" (*ISV*). I knew that after Newton's death, the government stepped in and stole the wealth from his estate to pay for it's own debts as they saw fit.

If it has happened to us, then it may very well have happened to you as well. Ask the Lord to reveal any wrongdoings that may have taken place in your lineage so that you can take the steps to align yourself with his will, in order to receive the restoration. Sometimes inheritances are right before us but there is something in our bloodlines that prevents us from obtaining it. Just like in the American court system, a will must be executed on the terms stating. Some of us have to first realize there is a will and further understand the instructions of the will. A will may have a clause that states the inheritance cannot be collected for one year, or the inheritance cannot be collected until a level of maturity is achieved. Seeking God and being obedient puts us in position to both receive what is ours as well as keep it.

ANCESTOR STONE PRAYER

I wrote this prayer out because I simply felt led to do so. I read it out loud a few times while I remained in the fast: I would encourage you to use it as guide. If you are being called, or led to a particular home, artifact or any other point of contact that may lead a legal inheritance, tweak it and ask to be spirit led in your prayer.

Heavenly Father we come before you Lord God and thank

endowed Newton with one of the greatest minds known to mankind; well versed in mathematics, science, technology, prophesy, and foreign language, Isaac Newton believed in you that the bible was coded with hidden blueprints for a greater plan. Just like it says it romans 12:6-8

"In his grace, God has given us different gifts for doing certain things well. So if God has given you the ability to prophesy, speak out as much faith as God has given you. If your gift is serving other, serve them well. If you are a teacher, teach well. If your gift is to encourage others, be encouraging. If it is giving, give generously. If God has given you leadership ability, take the responsibility seriously. And if you have the gift of showing kindness to others, do it gladly"(NLT).

Sir Isaac Newton believed that objects were endowed with sacred wisdom. Museum artifacts hold power in the recordings of their cellular structure. So as we lay our hands upon the mantle, we open ourselves to receive your blessing and family inheritance, the birthright that has been stored up and waiting for activation for almost three centuries. Praise be to the holy, and mighty name of Jesus. We receive father God. Thank you Lord. In Jesus name, amen!

CHAPTER 8

CLAIM

So the day finally came when we were to head up to Massachusetts to visit the college and get a tour of the library housing the reconstructed fore-parlor that belonged to Newton. The excitement of heading to the college was underscored with both the fact that my seven-day fast was nearly complete, as well as a taking off half a day of work! My parents, sister, and I all piled into a car and headed north for what was supposed to be a three-hour ride, as our New England home is approximately three hours from Boston. The college is advertised as being close to the states capital city, so we figured it would be a simple drive up the interstate.

The four of us were surprised, however, to see that the destination did not register in the vehicle's built-in GPS. The address did not seem to even exist! Each of us tried plugging in the destination in the GPS of our cell phones, however we wound up with three separate routes to three different locations. Over four and half hours later we found ourselves driving in circles through a tiny Massachusetts town attempting to decipher the GPS conundrum—so much for making an appointment.

It should go without saying that four strong minded people in a car for that many hours who are lost do not get along very well, and the spirit of strife began to try and work its way into the mix somewhere around the Massachusetts border. That is to be expected, though, considering the fact that when about to step into a new level in Christ, the enemy panics and tries its best to derail.

The enemy is a very clever and sneaky serpent. When you are set to hit a grand slam, naturally he is going to pull his pitcher and throw in an ace reliever to try and strike you out. The key is to always be vigilant and mindful of this. Resistance and curve balls will always come even when they were not invited to the party. Knowing your authority to take dominion over these attacks will allow you to enter into the places you are supposed to and not be held up in an unnecessary battle.

In effort to combat this in our own situation, we recognized the issue and rebuked the angry spirit. Listening to praise and worship music, as well as some anointed teachings the entire car ride help to end the demonic strategy. As we made conscious choices to end the foul spirit from disrupting our journey, it was as if we would receive little confirmations from signs and billboards. Once in particular that I remember read plainly, "turn a journey into accelerated rewards." These slogans and advertising campaigns were dotted along the highway like fortunes from inside of a Chinese cookie. As silly as that sounds, we seemed to notice signs and quotes that felt like positive affirmations. This journey was about to yield tremendous rewards.

After some time driving aimlessly around the suburbs of Boston, we asked for a solution. Our travels led us onto a quiet street where we saw a smiling UPS man standing outside of his delivery truck. Relieved, we pulled up and asked him for directions and debriefed him on our GPS troubles. With a chuckle he told us that the college was its own zip code separate from the town we were in and therefore did not show up on GPS navigation. He also told us that the roads to get there were very confusing and that it would be impossible to explain. He then told us to wait a second as he went to his truck and dug out an old map book from under his seat. Oh, the irony and metaphoric parallel to using a map to find the treasure. Certainly God has a sense of humor.

The route was indeed quite convoluted. With much generosity, the UPS representative even offered to have us follow him if we wanted him to lead the way. We declined but thanked him for the help because we were doing so well driving aimlessly through cities, we could figure it out ourselves. "What can brown do for you?" Another helpful slogan courtesy of the UPS!

I think it is really funny how far we are in terms of technological advancements and satellite GPS systems, yet it took a map to find this place just like it would have three hundred years ago. A lot of credit goes to the UPS driver who was gracious enough to help us. I suppose you can trust some men in short shorts.

UNLOCK AND LOCK

The pristine campus was quiet and seemed uninhabited. A

far cry from the busy metropolitan university I envisioned. Driving around the buildings and halls, we eventually found the library, which was very near to closing time considering how long it took us to find the place. Prior to going inside, the four of us spent a few minutes praying together in the car and reading aloud the prayer that had been given to me when I fasted. Once we said our amens, we made our way to the front desk. It was Friday evening and the administration was gearing up to head out and enjoy the weekend; fortunately, we coasted in before they split and were openly greeted with warm hospitality. Finally, the moment we had been preparing weeks for had come.

After the brief formalities and greetings with our escort, we were then ushered up to a floor closed off to students and the general public through an administrators-only elevator. As the elevator ascended, I thought about the angels waiting inside of the room. Were there cherubim inside of the reconstructed fore-parlor assigned to stand guard and watch over this treasure—a treasure that has been hidden in plain sight for so long? Did time move any faster or slower for these militant beings as they stood in complete obedience awaiting this day? A day when someone would come to collect what rightfully belonged to them?

I wondered if these angels were as excited as I was, knowing that what we were there to pick up what the angels had been commissioned the task of protecting for centuries. Perhaps these same angels who were sent to protect the mantle would then follow us along our new journey as part of our angelic support. Part of me wondered if they even knew, or were aware that they were about to be given new marching orders. Certainly this must have been an exciting time for both them and us! And just think, right now there are angels standing guard and anticipating the moment *you* discover what is hidden in plain sight from your lineage, just waiting to be legally claimed by the rightful beneficiary.

Stepping out of the elevator and heading down a corridor led us to the large oak door of the Newton room. The room itself was reconstructed inside what seemed to be a giant walk in museum vault. Viewers had to enter through a very thick museum glass door, which led into the actual wooden doorframe from Newton's house. Beyond that led into the fore-parlor: a room of antiquity beholding centuries of conversations and adventure. The room was large and had the smell of aged oak and a faded stain to go along with it. The paneled walls had old paintings and various portraits of Sir Isaac Newton, whose face carried some similarity to my father's facial features. In the back corner sat another door, closed, that seemed to blend in with the panels of the room. Had there not been a doorknob, one might not see it right away.

Two windows at either end of the room looked out over the flags of the nations that flew outside of the room on the building's roof. Laughing to myself I was reminded of a week or so prior when driving from Hazleton, Pennsylvania back to Connecticut after a wrestling event. For nearly the entire three and a half hour ride, I had been prophesying over my family. The car ride was an energetic trip that included a good half hour of calling out the flags of the nations and leaders of the world as an audience to hear the message and the word of the Lord that he has been given to our family to go forth and speak. An image of the waving flags popped into my mind as I spoke it. That same image I saw in my mind matched what my natural eyes saw outside of the right window. The confirmation of seeing these flags waiving outside of the window cemented in my mind the possibility of leaders and nations who would hear this message and be moved in the spirit.

At the far end was another original door next to the fireplace and mantle. Walking around the room and thinking "if these walls could talk" gave actual meaning to the saying. Seeing the ornate woodwork that ordained the walls of the room, one would be impressed and surprised that they were able to survive the ravenous flames of a house fire.

An attendant graciously allowed us private access, leading us in single file. Being the courageous one of the family, I bravely stepped in first and wasted no time absorbing the anointing inside. Stretching out my hands, I slid them across the right and left frame of the door entering into the old room. An immediate, and overwhelming sensation of my chest being opened and filled with light overtook me. Although a hard feeling to articulate into words, the feeling was quite pleasant and filled me with a sort of joyous energy. A supernatural wind opened up my chest. My intoxicated mind of euphoric happiness was elated as the renewing wind filled my body. No longer were there hunger pangs and headache symptoms from the week long fast.

The woman who was giving us the tour was talking about the history and timeline of the room and had no idea what was happening. She seemed slightly nervous and tense. One might say that her spirit was aware of the transference but her body had no idea how to react to the heightened spiritual activity taking place right before her eyes, despite the innocent appearance of four people running their fingers across the walls.

Nodding along as our escort chattered on and on, euphoria settled on me in a heavy manner. Lean on the wooden conference table, I focused on the glory that was filling the atmosphere. After a while, the guide seemed to run out of things to say and told us to feel free to walk around and look at everything. Standing up from a leaning position on the table, I turned around and looked at the mantle above the fireplace at the opposite end of the long room. "Well there it is" escaped my mouth as each of us made our way towards it. The mantle was my purpose for going. The narrow wooden shelf was the point of contact that was built up in my mind and imagination to use as transference of anointing.

Reaching up, I placed my hands on the mantle and instantly felt light headed. At the same moment a shot of freezing cold energy went down my back and my internal temperature shot through the roof. My upper body got very warm very quickly. Immediately there was a sensation of freefalling backwards and despite leaning forward and holding onto the mantle. There was brief moment when I let go and stood looking up at the giant painting of Newton. The pursed lips and paternal expression of wisdom struck me as fluttering gold swirls unraveled in front of eyes. Transference had occurred.

Walking around the room and running my hands and fingers along the walls and window frames, I was determined to absorb whatever was waiting to be claimed. Not even the floor was left untouched. Kneeling down, I felt the old floorboards and ran my fingers across the grain of the wood. You name it I touched it. No stone was left unturned in that room to make sure that every drop of anointing was picked up! The guide probably thought we were nuts walking around putting our fingerprints on everything, but that is ok. That's what Pine Sol is for.

Back near the painting of Sir Isaac Newton that was hanging above the mantle and to the left, was the window with the flags as well as the second door. The beautiful old door was ornamented with an old black iron lock. The guide said to me "that door is locked because it does not lead to anything anymore." Unphased by this, I touched the lock and said out loud, "Release in Jesus name. Unlock now, in the name of Jesus." A loud an audible "click" sound resonated inside of my head. It was at that precise moment when a sense of completion overtook me and I knew it was time to stop fingerprinting everything in the room.

Accessing the kingdom faith is necessary to succeed in situations like this. Putting faith and trust in Jesus and using him as the rampart to fortify trust is what gives us the ability to believe in things beyond what we are programmed in us as actuality. God is bigger than our understanding and when we call upon Jesus for understanding and assurance, things that seem unrealistic or impossible becomes absoluteness. This kingdom faith is a faith larger than ourselves and when we tap into it, we can operate beyond doubt in our expectation. Choosing to submit my understanding and allow the understanding of Jesus to act on my behalf was what allowed me to receive the transference. The shift was complete because the inheritance within our DNA was awakened through a legal claim in the birthright of our family. Not only had picked up the mantle of Sir Isaac Newton, as well as unlocked anything held up or frozen from obtaining the full inheritance, but we now carry that anointing into a new generation of discovery... wheels within wheels.

After a while of exploring and learning all about the room and its contents, we headed out. The thing that sticks in my mind was after we walked out, our guide left the thick glass museum door to the room open. As we were heading back down the green-carpeted corridor to the elevators at the end, my mother walked back and shut the glass door. Later, the four of us agreed that it was a necessary action in the natural, to seal off that which had no right or claim in the supernatural. Closing the door to the Newton room was an action that mirrored what I had done inside of the room by unlocking the inner door. My mother sealed off the exterior in order to prevent anyone or anything from trying to rob our family of this birthright again. The significance of this action is key because what is the sense of awakening an inheritance if you aren't going to seal up the access point from scavengers and thieves? You know the expression "What, do you live in a barn? Shut the door!"

The fine folks at the college presented us with official bound copies of Sir Isaac Newton's manuscripts and writings before we left. Books of collections that had been acquired and preserved through the school's efforts to house and curate the collection of Newtonia were given to us. The gesture was unexpected and very kind of our hosts. The four of us thumbed through the copies as we sat in a restaurant afterwards to break our fast. The only real tragedy to note was fasting for seven days only to end it with mediocre pizza.

I THINK HE WAS WEARING AN ASCOT

In the weeks that followed our little adventure, my parents, sister, and I would continue with a nightly prayer. Many hours were spent chatting and pressing into scripture. I wanted to know how much we had changed. Did we in fact awaken an anointing once carried by Sir Isaac Newton? The question was about to be answered in the most surreal way.

Once we begin to untangle from the lies and boundaries placed on our mind, we start to see change. What I mean by that is you as a person begin to accept nuances and obscurities once thought to be coincidence, or fiction, as actual truth. The ideology of "perhaps", or "maybe" changes to absolute. The very best example I can give you is what happened during one of these family prayers.

Let me just back up for a moment and say that if you have not or do not practice this kind of corporate prayer, it's ok. Although, it would be my recommendation that you get involved with a group in the church or somewhere else if not your own family, where you can exercise the power and breakthrough of group prayer. If you are serious about taking your walk to a new level, God will put the right people in your life. He will also remove people too! So, be committed to growing. For us, these family prayers were relatively new to our family. We had not practiced this for years and years. It was in its formative stages when we began to understand some of God's true nature, and is the reason why we often get together to press in as a family unit, rather than a solo act. God is a family man, and thus family prayer is equally important as alone time with him.

As I was saying, the best example I can give you of how

awakening our spiritual inheritance has increased my capacity to understand and see differently was during a family prayer. The four of us had been praying and talking about the possibilities of miracles described in scripture. We were trying to understand the science behind Jesus walking on water in the book of Matthew. Questions were raised as to how Jesus was able to slip threw an angry crowd trying to kill him in the book of John, or how he changed his appearance to attend the festival in John 7. Not only did we seek answers about the many amazing things Jesus was said to have done, but how did Peter escape from the prison in Acts 12? How did Phillip transport to Azotus? We wanted to understand these things.

And then, suddenly as a family, we time traveled.

Sconces with burning candles illuminated the wooden walls of the fore parlor room. Sitting in an uncomfortable chair I saw my father standing in front of us dressed like Ben Franklin! He was explaining the physics of teleportation while dressed like he belonged on the one-hundred-dollar bill!

Shaking my head and rubbing my eyes I questioned what it was I thought I was seeing. There was my old man standing in the middle of our living room explaining quantum theories to the four of us as if we were supposed to be taking notes. His entire countenance had changed as he enthusiastically explained why so and so did this, and why so and so did that. He was dressed in what I would best describe as a colonial looking outfit with gold buttons and a puffy shirt. He actually looked quite ridiculous. As he pushed the round spectacles on his nose closer to his eyes, they reverted back to the modern square frames he was wearing at the start of prayer and then back to antique round ones. The room seemed to be flashing back and forth from our living room in Connecticut to the ornate fore parlor of Sir Isaac Newton. It was totally mind bending.

After his lecture concluded, the room appeared to shift back to the stuffy familiar dimensions of my parents' living room in New England. The four of us looked at each other not knowing what had just happened. All at once we blurted out "did you see that!?" Dad, of course now dressed in his trusty flannel and golfing shorts stood there processing the last two minutes as he stood up straight from a slouched teaching pose. In a stunned voice I heard my mother say "We just translated."

Easily one of the most, if not the most incredible thing I have seen while not using drugs. For those few short moments, everything had aligned mentally, spiritually, physically, and supernaturally for the four of us. A charge surged throughout my body like my blood was electrified. The sensation was as if my body was plugged into an electric outlet, and my spirit lit up. The awareness was a familiar feeling, yet at the same time a totally new one, if that makes any sense. I believe our spirits connected with the anointing we picked up in the fore parlor and synchronized together to time travel back to the time when Newton entertained some of the brilliant minds of his era in his home. This of course sounds really nuts to admit, but at the same time nothing should surprise us even if it sounds wacky. To me, that means I'm on the right track.

Considering this phenomenon is all such a new experience

for modern Christians we have to realize that the enemy does not want us to reach our full potential. Centuries have passed since teachings of these anomalies were known. Spirituality has become watered down and replaced with religion in order to keep believers from operating in their rightful authority. When you step up and contend for your own jawbone if you will, you are choosing to lay claim to the mighty power of God. A power so spectacular, it cannot be measured in gold, silver, or even time! It's time we go back to the future!

It is my hope that you are inspired and encouraged to seek out what is hidden and waiting for you to claim for your life. You are chosen and called by name to do greater works. That should be an energizing realization for you to press forward and discover what God truly has in store for you. Ask the Lord to incite a rally in your heart that propels you to understand more of his goodness.

I invite you to repeat this prayer out loud if you want to know more of him in a way that yields a more personal relationship with him:

Father God I thank you for your goodness. I thank you that you love me enough to trade your son Jesus' life for my own. I thank you Jesus for coming to this earth to become the ultimate sacrifice so that I may live. I repent of my sins because I want to know more of you. And God I want to know more about me. Help me today to understand and walk out the calling you have on my life. I surrender my wants, needs, and cares to you so that I may become a vessel for you to dwell in. I accept your grace, not because I deserve it, but because you give it to me freely from your mercy seat. Help me today to discover more of my origin. Let me uncover the hidden truths and mysteries of your kingdom. Lord I want to move and operate on a level that this generation has not yet seen. Thank you for helping me today, in Jesus name, amen.

CHAPTER 9

IGNORANCE

You've made it through the time travel story, so let's talk about something even more offensive to religious spirits. A lot of false doctrines exist in Christianity, and even in some its variants, each having their own unique detours in relationship with God. Detours that lead you to go around and around on the same path getting you nowhere.

I CALL THEM "CHURCHIES"

I have a lot of favorite false doctrines, from the standing for scripture readings, getting whisked away naked into the night and never to be seen again on Earth (AKA the Westernized rapture theory), or my personal favorite, the ultimate Churchie known as a Jahovah's Witness.

You have to understand what I mean when I say "Churchie." A Churchie is someone who wears a mask of the goody-two-shoes, the most falsely pious of the lot. These are the people who claim to be religious but at the same time are perturbed by all the "works" they need to do "in Christ." They are, in fact just that—religious! We all know or have met an MDP, a Modern Day Pharisee. Churchies aren't to be confused with regular church-goers, these are the out of control believers who make it their mission to get everyone else just as saved as they are and usually by force.

Again, just to reiterate, I'm not attacking churchgoers because it's important to have fellowship and be around other believers. A Churchie takes the call a little too personal and enlists in the Good News Gestapo to police other believers who are just enjoying their freedom in Christ.

Now there's a section of Churchie Elite known as the Jahovah's Witness. I find it odd how they like to show up at our front door—and only our front door on the entire block. Ironically, and not to be braggadocious, but we have the elephant on the street and I have reason to believe that their choosing our house isn't because they can sense our fields are ripe for harvest.

They each have their own sales pitch when they knock on the front door, but my favorite was the most recent. I was met with a short woman with big teeth, pursed lips, and angry brow who answered my greeting with an already defeated "I didn't see a sign that said I couldn't come in." She stood on the porch with her partner in crime, a timid 17-year-old boy who nervously fidgeted with his clip-on tie.

Amused, I responded with "It's alright, we like to talk about Jesus."

She proceeded with her memorized greeting about being saved; being careful not to announce outright that she was a Jahovah's Witness. I put my hand up to just confirm that I was in fact talking to two Jahovah's Witnesses.

Again, defeatedly she replied a very tight "Yes."

I asked her, "Let me just get this straight, and correct me if I'm wrong. Your belief is based on the idea that only 144,000 of you will actually be saved and go to heaven?"

She said "Yes, well..."

And I said "So if you think about it, if you play those odds, you aren't going to make it. Why bother?"

This is what surprised me. Their belief has evolved into accepting a Plan B. Knowing that her and her rookie aren't going to be one of the fortunate 144,000, they've accepted the belief that they're going to be part of the larger remnant who will inherit a perfect Earth that will be restored to where God intended it to be.

So I said, "Why would you devote your life to a God who doesn't love you enough to let you join Him in paradise, but rather keeps you separate from Him for all of eternity?"

She said, "Well we're not separate, He lives within me and I talk to Him every day."

And I asked, "But do you know him?"

"Well he lives in me," she replied.

"But have you met him?" I said.

She said, "Face to face?"

And I said, "Yes."

"That's impossible."

"Is it?"

"The Bible says if you look at God face to face," she replied, "you'll die."

I said "That's false doctrine and it's a wrong interpretation. Look at the examples of people in the Bible who saw God's face and didn't die."

And that's when she checked out. It was too much. She just couldn't comprehend what I had just said to her.

"The God I know and love," I explained, "loves me enough to love me back. My God doesn't want to be separate from me and would never shun me to live out eternity on another planet. What kind of God is that?"

And sadly, that's exactly what some of us Christians have done to God. In our own ignorance, we've false theologies that keep us separate from intimate relationship and moving in the fullness of our divine inheritance. One small idea of not being able to see God face to face, not being able to do all of the things Jesus did, even the wacky stuff, actually creates within us a false doctrine.

Jesus time traveled. He was born around 0 A.D., but is credited as wrestling with Jacob, met with Samson's parents in Judges 13, and met with Abraham before moving onto Sodom & Gomorrah. David wrote in his Psalms an eyewitness account and play-by-play witness of Jesus at the cross. John the revelator ascended up into heaven and witnessed the things to come. Moses ascended up Mount Sanai and was shown in great detail creation through up until the time he was in at that point. All of these men time travelled. If time travel is offensive, then disbelief in that possibility or ability can lead to a false understanding of who we are in Christ and what our inheritance is both *in* and *with* Him.

The supernatural is offensive to many—but especially in Christians. It isn't the scientists who disbelieve in quantum physics, sci-fi, time and space travel. It's the Christians! Let's just think about what causes the offense; a religious spirit. And what might be the purpose of a religious spirit? To hold people captive and limit what it is they are to do here on the Earth. If doubt and unbelief has caused your walk to be stunted and ineffective, then the enemy has won. Each of us has many supernatural things to do written on our scrolls, but the easiest way to deter us from completing them is to first convince us that the supernatural is demonic, or worse, doesn't exist.

Claiming your inheritance is a lot more than having some money or assets credited to your accounts. Your inheritance reaches far beyond your natural means. It's about a supernatural lifestyle, moving and doing things for the Kingdom. It's about leading the world in the ancient paths. And further, it's about having a really personal relationship with God where all things *truly* are possible.

FREEDOM FROM RELIGION

As I go forth with this new assignment, I am thankful that God has given me the strength, as well as the angelic support needed, to spread this message throughout the world. I am thankful to be the confirmation needed to others who have heard from the Creator. This is a new territory for the church that has been hidden and demonized for too long. Many lies and boundaries have been erected over the centuries that intentionally block the gifts that are rightfully ours to inherit. Religion is what keeps us from knowing the love and power of God. Religion replaces our father with parameters and limitations that only have the power to restrict **you**.

America, specifically, has trouble with the concept of spirituality, despite much of the programming on television being supernaturally based. The issue is that it focuses on weak channels and impure content. Much of the programming emphasizes the possibility of communicating with the dead. I always wondered why people are so apt to tune into something that tries to connect with that which is dead when they could be trying to connect with the living God. All over the world, people accept and recognize the fact there is a spirit realm layered over this physical world we perceive. In some countries, the spirit realm is even celebrated through pagan festivals and demonic commemoration. America seems to be the only nation that turns away and will only acknowledge stylized entertainment.

I used to work with a man from Jamaica years ago. For the sake of privacy, I'll say his name was Davion. Davion was a world traveler, living in each country for short stints before moving to the next. The two of us worked together on a loading dock for a national retailer. During our shifts on the loading dock which mainly comprised of us lifting heavy televisions and refrigerators, we dock grunts took turns blasting music at obscene levels from the company provided stereo. One fellow in particular preferred black death metal that would cause Davion to become very uncomfortable— sometimes made worse by me pestering him about what it was that caused him such discomfort. "Bad feelings in the air mon," he would say, "very evil tings." He was a seer for sure, something I was familiar with but not to the extent of Davion's experience.

There were many stories Davion reluctantly shared with me. Many of which sounded like they were out of a horror show. Judging by the look in his eyes and the strict abhorrence of certain music, these stories were anything but fiction in Davion's world. One time we talked about his experiences in Jamaica that sent shivers up my spine. Davion told me in all seriousness about witnessing a grown man who practiced voodoo, transform into a giant snake right before his eyes and slither up a tree. He could still hear the bones cracking and popping as the man snake coiled up into the high branches. Apparently this type of phenomenon is not as shocking to locals. I, however, was floored.

Davion also told me was that during his time in Mexico, where they celebrate the Day Of The Dead, he watched evil spirits run around and jump onto people's backs. These creatures tormented people like some sort of a bizarre, piggyback rodeo. Instead of bulls, the entities harassed and rode on top of humans. I would badger Davion constantly because these stories seemed outlandish and completely far out. One day I asked him how he wound up at this lousy loading dock in Connecticut. After all, he has lived all over the world. Why stay here? Davion told me that he preferred living in America because the people in the states, for the most part, refuse to acknowledge the spirit world. Therefore, it was easier for demons to hide and get away with whatever they wanted. He felt that even though he knew they were around, they appeared less often and he felt safer not having to see them all the time.

Davion was the first person I ever heard who talked about an atmospheric shift, and he was not even a Christian. You do not have to be a believer in Christ in order to feel the power of the supernatural. You do need to know the Lord and cultivate the spirit of discernment to navigate through what is and is not a clean channel. Davion was seeing clearly what exists in the spirit realm. He witnessed demons performing whatever their assignment was and it frightened him. I used to think that America was one nation under God.

That was why we do not see as much of the evil spirit activity manifesting.

One day I heard the word "rebellion." I contemplated it and realized that America was formed, in some ways, under a rebellious spirit—one of freedom from religion. Our history touts that we wanted freedom from England in order to practice whatever religion we wanted, as well as to be free from the taxation of the crown. Now days, America is what they call a "melting pot" of culture (also with heavy taxation). We are free to worship whatever God we wish or choose to not worship at all. It really is a rebellious spirit against the one true God, the Lord Jesus Christ. That is why there are pillars set up all over the country that look like the Washington monument. They are just concrete Asherah poles. This country presents itself as a Christian nation. I wish that were the case, but I really don't agree that it is.

Perhaps I will see it from a different perspective someday when the church awakens to its full and rightful authority. Right now, I see a country that acknowledges the power of lesser principalities posing as a supreme deity. There is only one Alpha and Omega, though, and America does not as a whole, acknowledge that anymore. That is why I believe it is easier for the enemy to move about and search for those he wants to devour, all with limited resistance.

Unfortunately, the life of a believer who recognizes the reality of a supernatural world is not always ice cream and candy, or grape juice and crackers for that matter. There is a very real and active realm of supernatural forces that does not want you to fulfill your destiny and awaken your spiritual inheritance. Fortunately, our God is bigger and stronger. You'll be just fine.

CHAPTER 10

FINALITY

One of the struggles we have as the Western Church is to overcome some of the Greek thinking that we have in regards to the Kingdom. A lot more revolves around being a follower of Christ than Church on Sunday and praying the sinner's prayer. Paul tells us that we are continually working our own salvation, and praying the salvation prayer is not the end of the Christian road, it's only the beginning. Some have made it their mission to stay there. And that's ok, I mean if that's what you want that's what you'll get. But if you want more of God, more of the Kingdom, more of what He paid the price for us to have, well, you'll just have to step out of your comfort zone.

TREASURES OF DARKNESS

I know that myself and others who have been on this journey have been chosen to be the confirmation of others hearing this message. This is brand new territory for the body of Christ. The kingdom of the Lord is so much bigger than any box one would try to stuff him in. Think about this,

Jesus was sealed in a tomb! It did not work so well, he was out in a few hours.

Backlash is the price paid for taking a stand and choosing not to shy away from your beliefs, specifically convictions that do not match up with the norm. There are some subjects that have not been taught purposely for thousands of years. Just accept that there are always going to be those who come against it and who are offended. The bible tells us clear as day in John 15: 18-21:

> "If the world hates you, know that it has hated me before it hated you. If you were of this world, the world would love you as its own; but because you are not of the world, but I chose you out of the world, therefore the world hates you. Remember the word I said to you: 'A servant is not greater than his master.' If they persecuted me, they will also persecute you. If they kept my word, they will also keep yours. But all these things they will do to you on account of my name, because they do not know him who sent me." (*ESV*)

You will never experience the sort of reward that separates the haves from the have not's without taking a risk. Leaps of faith! Nehemiah 13:2 tells us that our God is very capable of turning a curse into a blessing. So keep this in mind when the inevitable lazy Christians and elitist atheists start the smear campaign. "But he knows where I am going. And when he tests me, I will come out as pure gold"(NLT).

I will be absolutely transparent with you. Your own ego

will get in the way. Many people have been brought up in a twisted and entangled mess of the gospel. Of course, not all of it is wrong. There are a lot of people out in the world who just do not have a clue of the true nature and power of Jesus. Even writing this book, a few times I stopped and thought long and hard about the content. Part of me was saying that this sounds very far out. It cannot really be of God can it? Like I said, there are some pretty far out ideas about things that on the surface seem anything but religious. I am reminded that that is a good thing, because religion is very often the problem! I still have to stop myself and realize that some of the things I was raised to believe are nothing more than false doctrines and failed teachings that produce zero fruit.

Remember, look around and determine if you are where you want to be. Are you experiencing the things that are promised? If not, I urge you to press in deeper to God and get direction to where he is trying to lead you.

I took the entire year of 2014 to sit and re-read the bible cover to cover. I sat alone in a quiet place everyday and read each and every single line slowly. I wanted to wipe out any presuppositions I had about God and what is written about him. I wanted to break away from all of the things I had been taught ever since I was a child. *I wanted to think for myself.*

During my study time I asked God to speak to me and help me understand what is written that actually made sense to me. Sometimes I would hear contradictory teachings from pastors on certain subjects and I would get confused. How can these pastors all be hearing differently and teaching opposite messages on the same principle? I took the year to stop listening to others and started to listen to how God was speaking to me. In that time, I have begun to see things from a point of view that is so much more open to the reality of how supernatural the Bible actually is. By studying what the Bible really says and spending time with the One whom it is about, I can better use my gift of discernment.

I see the Bible as a supernatural manifesto of not only things that happened, but of things that can still happen. The bible is full of the superpowers I read about as a child. Scripture tells us about people who did all sorts of miraculous things. There are people who operated in supernatural anointing and gifts that once seemed impossible to me. When I read about a giant killer, or a man with superhuman strength, I want to see that happen now. Reading about a king who is beyond genius levels of intellect, or men who never actually die, I want to be one of them. A few of these folks disappear and reappear. Like I said earlier, some guys get translated from one place on the earth to another. Diseases that have no cure are cured. Illnesses are abolished. The elements of the earth obey the words spoken over them—the Bible is the most fantastic thing I have ever read! I want to see these things happen now in my own life; reading about how it was the norm two thousand years ago is not good enough. That is why I believe in the possibility and reality of claiming what is locked inside of our DNA.

I really believe that if a person is serious about aligning himself back in sync with God, he or she has to put in the work. It is not an easy path, by any means. Such a path takes determination and persistence. The diligence required in maintaining a proper work ethic is necessary in order to achieve the full benefits of the kingdom. A person can miss their calling if they choose to ignore the signs and voice within. Call it intuition, conscience, "gut feeling," call it whatever you want. I call it the inner direction of the Living God who created us to live out our destiny.

Many people just want the end result yet ignore the work that is involved with experiencing a prosperous bounty. We live in a tumultuous world. We live in a time where our leaders are corrupt. Many of the principles and beliefs that make us believers are under attack. The good news is that history repeats itself and this has always been the case. Although we may be walking in the midst of a chaotic and unpleasant time, that does not mean we have to be victim to it because none of this is a surprise to Jesus.

My belief is not that we are subject to the punishment of a sinful culture. Much of the world, including America, openly rejects the God of Israel. Similarly, being a Christian has become quite unpopular. The enemy is trying to get believers to cower and hide—or even worse, become complacent and comfortable. He does not want a high-powered kingdom offense to become aware of its capabilities. Those with Kingdom faith should not be persuaded to hide and fall back into a retreat. Now more than ever, we should be pressing in and openly declaring the word of Jesus Christ!

Our calling is to become the light of the world, not in religious judgment of others and tearing down structures from within. After all, people are already being torn down and beaten by the governing laws of the supernatural. Believers do not need to finish the job. The dark principalities have an easy time controlling those who are not plugged into the Lord. So, when you become that illuminating beacon of Christ, those who do not know the power of God will want to know why you are prosperous.

They want to know what makes you invulnerable to the destruction of the wicked. So many families are torn apart, finances depleted, increasing unemployment, and faith dwindling. Now is the time to break free from the snares and entanglement of the enemy and to seek a deep cleansing of your bloodline and realignment with the DNA of Jesus and break off the tethers that have held us captive.

We as a body need to get grounded in the heavenly realm so that it resonates and comes into agreement with the earthly realm. The time is now to unlock all that is piled up in the heaps and storehouses of your inheritance. We are called to rise above the distraction, and limitations of a fallen world so that we are fully able to assume our rightful authority.

As a child of the living God, we are endowed with gifts and abilities that no other person in history will ever have. Learning what your objective is and seek the Lord for guidance is critical. Developing the intimate relationship that is available for us to have with God is the pathway to fulfilling our destiny. He will share his secrets and provide an understanding of the ways of the supernatural. Isaiah 45:30 says "And I will give thee treasures of darkness, and hidden riches of secret places, that thou mayest know that I, the LORD, which call *thee* by name, *am* the God of Israel" (*KJV*).

There is so much more in this life than a one-dimensional realm. What we see is not all that exists. Accessing these dimensions through the blood of Jesus will enable us as believers to access the keys needed to unlock our spiritual inheritance and awaken the sleeping giants hidden in our DNA. The time is now to bear up arms, cleanse the sin of our generations, and thank the Lord for a glorious victory over the restrictions of this world.

Pressing into the Word of God and stepping out in faith will take us far beyond our comfort zone and into the calling that is upon your life. You were made for victory! The battle is not won in your own strength, but by the might of the Spirit. Awaken the sleeping giants inside of you, for now is the time to slay the Philistines.

A BIT ABOUT JOHNNY

After spending many years working as an astutely recognized New York Times chef and moonlighting on the weekends as a bombastic manager in the world of professional wrestling, Johnny Newton is now the host and writer of the Curfew Show. His calling was realized after a series of missteps that led him on the right path towards fulfilling his destiny. Curfew Show serves as a catalyst in spreading Johnny's personal vision and seeing change in the body of Christ to acknowledge, activate, and advance the hidden places of the supernatural. Tired of running from his preordained path, Johnny was awakened by the Holy Spirit to step into his position as a mouthpiece for the Creator.

"...My tongue is the pen of a skillful writer" - Psalm 45:1

Johnny is a dynamic speaker who uses his wit, personal experience, and Kingdom authority as a launchpad to help believers realign themselves with the fullness of a living God. When he isn't speaking to those desiring a deeper conscious of God's infinity, Johnny courageously endures the bitter Connecticut winters.

LISTEN TO THE SHOW
LIVE GUESTS | COMEDY | MUSIC

CURFEW
WITH
Johnny Newton

CURFEWSHOW.COM

Connect with us and join the conversation!

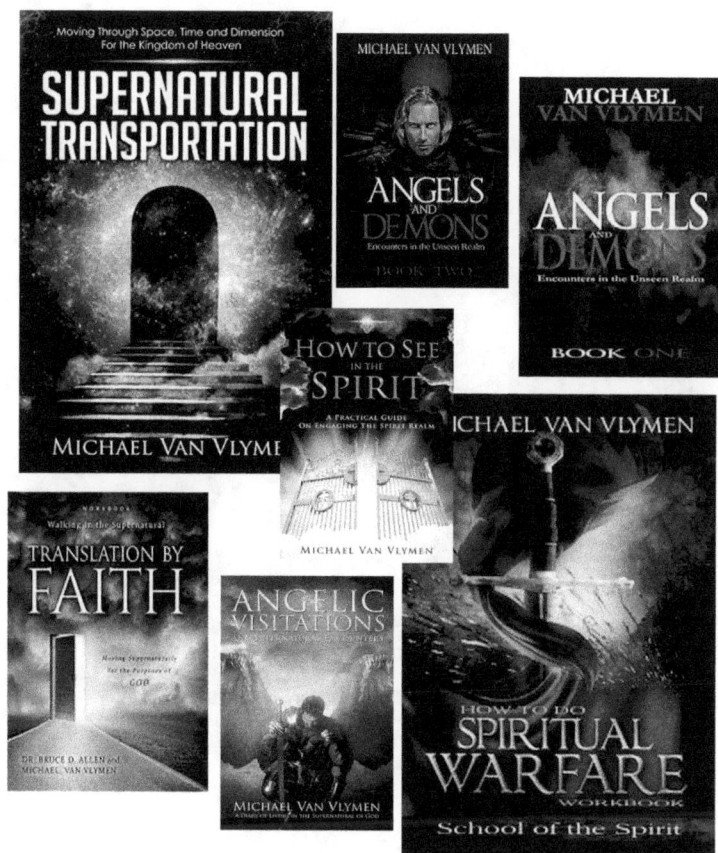

SPECIAL THANKS TO
JOAN HUNTER

JOANHUNTER.ORG

SPECIAL THANKS TO
SHAWN MORRIS

SHAWNMORRIS.ORG

NOTES

NOTES

NOTES